THE SECRET STRENGTH OF
ANGELS

Also by Frederic Flach, M.D.

THE SECRET STRENGTH OF DEPRESSION

RESILIENCE

A NEW MARRIAGE, A NEW LIFE

PUTTING THE PIECES TOGETHER AGAIN

RICKIE

THE SECRET STRENGTH OF
ANGELS
7 VIRTUES TO LIVE BY

FREDERIC FLACH, MD, KHS

FOREWORD BY
JANICE T. CONNELL
AUTHOR OF ANGEL POWER AND MEETINGS WITH MARY

hatherleigh

ᐳᐳᐳ hatherleigh

5-22 46th Avenue, Suite 200
Long Island City, NY 11101
www.hatherleighpress.com

Hatherleigh Press is committed to preserving and protecting the natural resources of the Earth. Environmentally responsible and sustainable practices are embraced within the company's mission statement.

Hatherleigh Press is a member of the Publishers Earth Alliance, committed to preserving and protecting the natural resources of the planet while developing a sustainable business model for the book publishing industry.

PEA Member   Earth-Friendly Printing

Earth-Friendly Printing: The interior of this book was printed with soy ink.

The Library of Congress has cataloged the hardcover edition as follows:

Flach, Frederic F.
  The secret strength of angels / by Frederic Flach.
    p. cm.
  Includes bibliographical references.
  I. Conduct of life. 2. Angels—Miscellanea. I. Title.
BJ 1581,2.F557 1998
1581. 1—dc21

  ISBN 1-57826-018-3
  ISBN 13: 978-1-57826-282-3

All Hatherleigh Press titles are available for bulk purchase, special promotions, and premiums. For more information, please contact the manager of our Special Sales Department at 1-800-367-2550

Interior design by DC Designs
Cover design by Andrew Flach and Pauline Neuwirth,
Neuwirth & Associates, Inc.

Printed in the United States of America

10 9 8 7 6 5 4 3 2 1

To my guardian angel,
who, I am sure, has frequently
had to work overtime
on my behalf

Contents

For he shall give his angels charge over thee, to keep thee in all thy ways.

Psalms 91:11

Every man hath a good and a bad angel attending on him in particular all his life long.

The Anatomy of Melancholy
ROBERT BURTON

Foreword

The late Frederic Flach, an imminent physician, well-known psychiatrist, and dedicated Knight of the Holy Sepulchre, had a lifelong relationship with his guardian angel. In this book, he examines seven known qualities all angels share and suggests ways for humans to develop their own capacities by emulating the angels.

Having studied and written extensively about angels myself, I find Dr. Flach's insights helpful and challenging. In the dawn of the era of global communication, what messages could be more valuable than those received directly from angels?

Dr. Flach combines his extensive medical and psychiatric knowledge with theology to present a unique approach to accessing the power of the angels.

Janice T. Connell, J.D., D.M.
Author of *Angel Power* and *Meetings with Mary*

Preface

Dear Reader,

My father believed in angels, and his favorite movie was the classic *It's a Wonderful Life.* For those of you who may not know it, the film tells the story of a man named George Bailey. He faces a major life crisis that causes him to wish he had never been born. His Guardian Angel, Clarence, is sent down from Heaven to help George and in turn earn his wings.

The script features the line: *Every time a bell rings an angel gets his wings.*

This is true: When my father died almost two years ago, it was my responsibility to see that he was honored in death as the good man he was: a knight, a healer, a philosopher, a man ahead of his time—an angel.

At the funeral home on the day of the service, my sister and I said a prayer and a goodbye. I chose to personally close the casket. Gently and evenly I lowered the casket lid. Precisely at the moment I secured the latch on my father's coffin, a bell rang.

Every time a bell rings an angel gets his wings.

The bell kept ringing. Loudly. Again and again. It was the stately clock that stood in the corner. My sister and I were astonished, but not surprised.

Every time a bell rings an angel gets his wings.

Dad, you have indeed earned your wings.

For those of you who read this book, I do hope you believe in angels. If not yet, maybe this book will shed light on those unexplainable moments in your life where perhaps your angel intervened. If you flatly deny angels, well, you can still learn a lot from the wisdom in this book. Keep an open mind. There is more that we don't know than we do know. Perhaps your angel has worked silently at your side throughout your life. I believe so.

Andrew Flach, Publisher

THE SECRET STRENGTH OF
ANGELS

Why Angels?

I

Why Angels?

In which you will learn why I take angels seriously

I HAVEN'T THOUGHT much about angels during my lifetime—not until recently, that is. My mother's middle name was Angela, and she was in many ways like an angel. I've thought about God, yes. And saints, and prayer, and Jesus Christ. But not angels, except humorously, as when early on in my medical career I used to give angels credit for my remarkable luck at finding places to park in New York City.

Looking back, I realize that I may owe my life to angels. When I was twenty-three, I was sailing in the Caribbean, off the coast of Cuba, when my small boat capsized. A friend and I had taken it from the Havana Yacht Club and foolishly went out too far, without having the sense to wear life jackets. Sail and rudder were gone. With great effort we hauled ourselves inside and sat there, water up to our waists, helpless. A burst of wind came up, and the next thing we knew we were clinging to the gunnels of the submerged boat. It was too far to swim ashore. Besides, the waters were full of sharks. Night was coming on fast. We were drifting in a swift current, southeastwardly, along the coast. Before long it was pitch black. I was shaking inside with fear, not knowing how we would ever be found in the darkness, not being sure how long the boat would stay afloat. My hopelessness only intensified when a brightly lit dance boat passed only a few hundred feet from us, the mambo drums drowning out our cries for help, and then disappeared from sight. I prayed, harder and more persistently than I had ever prayed. I thought, Please, God, let us live and I will do my best to serve you well. Hour after hour passed. I don't know how much time had gone by when my companion screamed in pain. An *aqua mala*, a Portuguese man-of-war, had brushed across his belly, its poison leaving a wake of angry welts. He kept talking about jumping overboard and, as I recall, my attention was diverted from my own desperation to talking to him about anything I could think of to try to get his mind off his anguish. But I felt it was hopeless. In the morning, if we lasted until then, the powerful sun would come out and within a few hours burn us to a crisp.

The sun rose innocently enough, golden over green hills that reminded me of Vermont. We were still about a mile from shore, and still afloat. In the distance I could see a large ship lumbering in our direction. I felt excited. Had they seen us? Yes. They had. The ship was moving unwaveringly toward us, and as it grew closer I could read the large letters painted on its side: Lehigh

Portland Cement. The sailors threw a ladder over the side, and one of them climbed down to help us up to the deck. They gave us hardtack and coffee, as the ship turned and headed back to harbor. We were safe, and already the nightmare began to assume the vague unreality of a dream. I said a prayer of thanks, reminding myself of my promises and determined to do my best to be faithful to them.

During that night, I was later told, my mother in New Jersey woke up, frightened by a premonition that something terrible had happened to me.

For years I remained convinced that my prayers had been heard by God. And recently I began to wonder whether God had not sent an angel to see us safely home.

Although much of what we know about angels comes from scripture and tradition, popular culture has a profound influence on how we perceive them. Movies, for example. As a teenager, several of my favorite films were about angels whose job it is to put things right. *Here Comes Mr. Jordan* stars Robert Montgomery as Joe Pendleton, a prizefighter who is killed in a plane crash. But his death is premature. It wasn't his time to die. There had been a bureaucratic mix-up in heaven. Claude Rains, as Mr. Jordan, and Edward Everett Horton are the angels who have to straighten things out. However, there's one problem. Joe's body has been cremated. So they have to find a new body for him to occupy. In the end, they do. But the story fascinated me; it didn't even seem far-fetched. That's the kind of reaction John Brain, author of *Room at the Top*, calls an essential ingredient of any good novel, namely, a reader's, or in this instance a viewer's, willingness to suspend disbelief. (The film, incidentally, won an Academy Award for the best original screen play of 1941.)

In another of my favorites, *The Bishop's Wife*, the angel's mission is to help salvage someone's spirituality. It stars David Niven as the bishop, Loretta Young as his wife, and Cary Grant as a handsome and urbane angel named Dudley. The bishop is so busy raising money from his wealthy congregation that he fails to notice his family life coming apart. When it is almost too late, in response to his prayers, Dudley arrives to help the bishop regain his sense of spiritual purpose and becomes, for a while, the object of his wife's genteel love. But when Dudley's mission is completed, he leaves, and neither the bishop nor his wife will have any memory of his having been around.

One of the most popular films during World War II was *A Guy Named Joe*, in which the angel's job is to help someone rebuild her life in the face of terrible tragedy. Spencer Tracy plays a pilot who is killed in action. He had been in love with a female pilot, played by Irene Dunne, who flew transports from America across the Atlantic to English airfields. Tracy returns as a ghost (not an angel) but acts like an angel, helping Van Johnson succeed as a flyer and encouraging Irene Dunne to accept Tracy's death and find a new life in love with Johnson.

But my favorite angel movie of all is about an angel who helps someone rediscover his own self-worth. It's Frank Capra's classic film *It's A Wonderful Life*. George Bailey, played by Jimmy Stewart, wishes he'd never been born. An angel, Clarence, played by Henry Travers, shows him what the world would be like had that been the case. George is then given a second chance. I think I've seen him running down the snow-covered street of Bedford Falls, shouting with joy and wishing everyone a Merry Christmas, a dozen times, yet it never fails to bring a tear to my eye. Am I sentimental? Sure. A believer in miracles? Of course.

It has dawned on me only recently that one of my favorite plays, T.S. Eliot's *The Cocktail Party*, which opened on Broadway in 1950, was about angels. And since the story involves a psychiatrist, Sir Henry Harcourt Reilly, played by Alec Guiness, it has particular relevance for me. By helping two people find meaning in their lives, Sir Henry is doing another task of angels. The two people, Edward Chamberlin and Celia Coplestone, have had an affair that is coming to a painful and disillusioning end. They encounter Sir Henry, who warns Edward that "I knew that all you wanted was the luxury of an intimate disclosure to a *stranger*... But let me tell you, that to approach the stranger is to invite the unexpected, release a new force, or let the genie out of the bottle. It is to start a train of events beyond your control." He subsequently convinces Edward to return to his wife. He offers Celia the possibility of a future that, for the very first time, can give her life meaning.

I was fascinated by the supernatural dimensions of the play. Seeing it undoubtedly reinforced my intent to become a psychiatrist, even though it hardly represented what day-to-day practice would really be like. Years later I even had the opportunity to meet Sir Alec at a friend's dinner party, where I told him of the powerful effect the play and his performance had had on me. Being a very spiritual man himself, he was evidently quite pleased. But it did not occur to me until I began to research this book that Sir Henry and his compatriots were probably meant to represent angels.

So, without being fully aware of it, I've been fascinated by angels most of my life. I can't say I have ever seen a glowing light or been helped by a stranger whom no one else seems to have seen. Every now and then, when I feel I am about to trip and fall, I feel a firm pressure on my arms that keeps me standing up. Maybe that's only because I have been actively working out with weights for several years now. But, then again, maybe not.

Looking back over my life, I can see a number of instances when angels may have come into play. These are moments when I experienced a sense of something or someone directing me, trying to tell me something, pushing me in one direction or another, illuminating me. One such moment was when I finally decided to remove my daughter Rickie from the care of psychiatrists and send her to a somewhat unconventional rehabilitation program where, after years of hospitalization, she recovered at last and has remained essentially well ever since. Rickie had been struggling with depression since she was thirteen years old. She also had a serious visual perception problem that had been completely undetected. She had been misdiagnosed as suffering with schizophrenia, and the best efforts of my colleagues only served to make her increasingly incapacitated. Now that I know more about angels, I must wonder whether, in answer to my prayers, and those of a lot of other people too, an angel helped to lead me to my discovery of a new and different path to follow for Rickie's sake.

I have long been impressed by Carl Jung's ideas about synchronicity. He suggested that seemingly random events may actually come together in a meaningful way, not following the ordinary laws of cause and effect as we understand them, but in a way that profoundly influences us and alters the direction of our lives. They seem to be coincidence, but they are far more interconnected than we can imagine. You almost don't go to a certain party, for example, but something inside you urges you to get up and get dressed and go. And, lo and behold, "across a crowded room" you see a man or a woman whom you meet, get to know as time goes by, fall in love with, marry, and with whom you have children and spend the rest of your life. It's as though you have chosen to follow God's plan for you. You could have decided to stay away. Who or what nudged you on? A guardian angel?

I had a patient once, a very attractive 29-year-old woman named Charlotte, who was depressed as a result of several very unhappy love affairs in which she had been betrayed or left profoundly disappointed. It was before the modern antidepressants were available, so I had to help her work through her anger and grief and regain her self-respect and confidence in herself through strictly psychological means. It took a couple of years all told. Near the end of our work together, she said, "I'm so much better now. In fact, for the first time in my life I feel ready for a real relationship. I want to get married and have children. But I feel my chances of meeting someone right are very thin."

"If you're ready, and it's what is meant for you, your chances of meeting someone special are very good," I replied.

A few months later, out of the blue, she received a letter from a man whom she had dated for a short time while she was still in college. He had been one of her teachers, ten years older than she. They both felt the age difference was too great for them to continue their relationship, so they reluctantly broke up. Now he was a widower with two small children, living in Europe, planning to return to America, and wanting to see her again. Within a year, they were married. The last I heard, they had two children of their own. If you believe in angels, you might think – especially consid-ering the timing – that one of them may have inspired him to write that letter....

    .... If you believe in angels.

II

Believing in Angels

For those readers who may have doubts about the existence of angels, and those who already believe but enjoy being reminded of why they believe

*T*HERE'S NOTHING that says you have to believe in angels. You certainly don't have to believe in them in order to get a great deal out of this book. But, if you believe that the Bible is the Word of God, you probably believe. As the Rev. Dr. Billy Graham puts it:

> I am convinced that these heavenly beings exist and that they provide unseen aid on our behalf. I do not believe in angels because someone has told me about a dramatic visitation from an angel, impressive as such rare testimonies may be. . . I do not believe in angels because of the sudden worldwide

emphasis on the reality of Satan and demons. I do not believe in angels because I have ever seen one – because I haven't.

I believe in angels because the Bible says there are angels; and I believe the Bible to be the true Word of God.

And even if you don't have such powerful faith in the Bible, you may believe because so many strange, inexplicable events have happened to people—maybe even to you—that you can account for only by admitting that something mysterious and beautiful and unseen is busily at work in the world helping us make it through the years.

Children of many faiths—Christian, Jewish, Moslem, Hindu—are taught that each of us has a guardian angel who follows us throughout life from birth to death. An image is conjured of an angel on your shoulder, standing straight and tall, ready to comfort, inspire, offer guidance and direction, instill courage, bolster your spirits when you're down, empathize with your pain and suffering, maybe even save your life if you're adrift in a rudderless sailboat in the Caribbean Sea.

It is at once obvious that angels are among the most ecumenical of creatures.

The idea of angels is ancient. Angels figure in Zoroastrianism, one of humankind's earliest attempts to shift from a polytheistic (many gods) to a monotheistic (one God) vision. Hebrew Scriptures and the New Testament contain important references to angels. When God banishes Adam and Eve from the Garden of Eden, an angel (said to be the archangel Michael) drives them out, and another angel is placed to guard the way to the tree of life so that they cannot return (Genesis 3:23–24). In Chapter 18 of Genesis, three strange men (angels, in fact) appear to Abraham and tell him that his wife, Sarah, who is elderly and barren, will bear him a son. And again in Genesis, Chapter 22, when the Lord tempts Abraham by ordering him to sacrifice his son, Isaac, it is an angel of the Lord who calls out to Abraham to stay his hand. In Daniel 3:24–28, it is an angel who rescues Shadrach, Meshach, and Abednego from the fiery furnace. In 2 Kings 19:3, "the angel of the Lord went out and put to death a hundred and eighty-five thousand men in the Assyrian camp" to protect Hezekiah and the Israelites. The angel Raphael guides Tobias on his dangerous journey into unknown lands (Tobias 5:4). Michael (the protector), Gabriel (the messenger), and Raphael (the healer; the term *rapha* in Hebrew means "healer," "doctor," or "surgeon") are named as three of the "seven holy angels who present the prayers of saints and enter into the presence of the glory of the Holy One." Uriel, Raguel, Sariel, and Fanuel are mentioned by name in the apocryphal books.

In the New Testament, it is the angel Gabriel (Luke 1:26–38) who goes to Nazareth and announces to Mary that she is to become the mother of Jesus. It is an angel appearing as a being of light who rescues Peter from prison (Acts 12:5–11). An angel clothed in a cloud appears to St. John the Divine in his vision of the end of the world (Revelations 10:1–11). During his agony in the Garden of Gethsemane, there appears to Jesus "an angel from heaven, strengthening him" (Luke 22:42–43). And at his resurrection, "an angel of the

Lord descended from heaven and came and rolled back the stone, and sat upon it. And behold. . .his appearance was like lightning, and his raiment white as snow. And for fear of him, the guards trembled and became like dead men" (Matthew 28:2–4). *Not exactly cherubic.*

Bothered by the paganism and idolatry of Mecca, Mohammed believed that it was the angel Gabriel who delivered the messages that were to constitute the core of the new faith of Islam. Joan of Arc, in the fifteenth century, attributed to the archangel Michael one of the voices that she heard directing her to save France. In this, the twentieth century, the Italian Roman Catholic priest Padre Pio reported numerous encounters with angels, and even suggested that people should consider sending their guardian angels to consult with him if they could not come themselves. Devas in the Hindu religious tradition are a kind of lesser god whose functions very much resemble those of angels, especially that of carrying messages from the higher gods to human beings.

Just because billions of people have believed in something since the beginning of time does not necessarily make it so. Nevertheless, in spite of the incredible scientific understanding of things that we have achieved, especially in modern times, we cannot prove that angels *don't* exist. I think, to be on the safe side, it's best to believe. Increase Mather was a Puritan who lived from 1639 to 1723. In his *Angelographia* he wrote: "Angels both good and bad have a greater influence on this world than men are generally aware of. We ought to admire the grace of God toward us sinful creatures in that He hath appointed His holy angels to guard us against mischiefs of wicked spirits who are always intending hurt to both our bodies and our souls." Whether angels are basically an archetype, a creation that serves our need to understand good and evil, and to have a powerful source of love and support, or whether there is an angel, right now, standing next to me and to you, in our own rooms, watching kindly over us, waiting for our prayers, we cannot help but consider that angels do indeed mirror the better part of ourselves.

One of the countrymen:
A welcome at the door to which no one comes?

The angel:
I am the angel of reality,
Seen for a moment standing in the door

I have neither ashen wing nor wear of ore
And live without a tepid aureole,

Or stars that follow me, not to attend,
But, of my being and its knowing, part,

I am one of you and being one of you
Is being and knowing what I am and know.

Yet I am the necessary angel of earth,
Since, in my sight, you see the earth again,

Cleared of its stiff and stubborn, man-locked set,
And, in my hearing, you hear its tragic drone

Rise liquidly in liquid lingerings,
Like watery words awash, like meanings said

By repetitions of half-meanings. Am I not
Myself, only half a figure of a sort,

A figure half seen, or seen for a moment, a man
Of the mind, an apparition appareled in

Apparels of such lightest look that a turn
Of my shoulder and quickly, too quickly, I am gone?

Angel Surrounded by Paysans
WALLACE STEVENS

III

What Do We Really Know About Angels?

For anyone who knows as little—or as much—as I do about angels, and for those who perhaps know a great deal more

WHAT ARE these creatures called angels? The word *angel* comes from Greek and means "messenger." Traditionally angels are seen as messengers between God and human beings, moving in both directions. We can only piece together our notions about what angels are, since we really do not know for sure.

Angels predate humankind. Before God created the earth (whether it took seven biblical days or seven billion human-time years), he created a realm of invisible spirits—angels, who are personal beings, whose purpose is to praise and adore him and serve him in various ways. They are thought to be characterized by light, and those who have reported seeing angels usually describe them as light. They also seem to have the power to assume human form. But since they are not material beings, when they do so it is as if they put on a costume so that they can be seen and heard, but their supernatural nature remains intact.

They are neither male nor female. They do not procreate. They have been given enormous intelligence, power, and free will. This explains how some of the angels (it is believed) under the leadership of an angel called Lucifer, defied God out of pride and were expelled from heaven and driven into hell, as well as here on earth, with their powers unfortunately intact. Good angels are wise, compassionate, courageous, and eager to give help wherever and whenever it is needed, and *especially when they are asked to do so*.

Angels are considered to be a higher order of creature than we humans. They do possess certain attributes that resemble our own, such as intelligence and will, but to a much greater degree. The fact that they are probably a quite different order of being than ourselves should not discourage us, however, from emulating them in ways in which we are able.

Joan Webster Anderson, in her book *Where Angels Walk*, asks the question, What do angels do? Well, we know they bring important news. "They open our eyes to moments of wonder, to lovely possibilities, to exemplary people. They lift our hearts. They sit silently with us as we mourn. They challenge us toward new understanding. Angels offer practical help. . . furnish information, provide food, buffer the storms of life. . ." Then she points out that "we can [also] do that for each other."

What do angels look like? We really can't say for sure. Nevertheless, people have a strong need to translate spiritual concepts into pictorial representations. We try to picture what God looks like, and what angels look like too. In some images angels are gentle and reassuring. In others they are powerful and determined. Then there are the round-faced cherubs flying through the air, playing on their harps. And Lucifer sometimes appears ridiculous, and sometimes like a child's worst nightmare, with fangs and horns, waving about a long, ugly tail.

It is important for us to consider how we imagine angels to be, because those images have a profound influence on whether or not we really want to be in any way like them. I mean, who wants to float through the air looking like a cherub? What "real" man, who enjoys John Wayne movies, wants to be seen in a flowing white gown, wearing wings?

Many of our notions about what angels look like come from art: the paintings of Rembrandt, Rubens, Michelangelo, Giotto, Albrecht Dürer, Raphael, and Fra Angelico. Giotto di Bondone (1267–1337) was perhaps the first artist to present an ideal representation of angels. In his *Mourning the Dead Christ*, he portrayed them as small, winged creatures with human features. In Fra Angelico's *Annunciation* (1440–1445), the angel possesses a more feminine appearance, whereas in Michelangelo di Lodovico Buonarotti Simoni's (1475–1564) *Last Judgment* in the Sistine Chapel, the angels are portrayed as more masculine, without wings, and looking very human.

The angels of Raphael Sanzio (1483–1520) in his *St. Michael Conquering Lucifer* are spiritual and graceful, the personification of intelligence and power, serious, majestic. Those in Cozzoli Benozzo's *Angels in Adoration*

(1497) cast their eyes down humbly; their hands are clasped in prayer; their countenances speak to a great sense of peace. In the painting of a study of Verrochio, in which the angel Raphael accompanies Tobias on his journey, the angel looks like a friend or companion, and the two figures appear to be carrying on a casual conversation. Angels are portrayed as powerful military figures in Luca Signorelli's fresco *The Apocalyptic Damned Cast into Hell* (1500–1504). The angel in Gustav Dore's *Jacob Wrestling with the Angel* (1855) looks very much like a real champion.

As for Lucifer, on the Fathers of the Church altar in Munich, Michael Pacher portrayed the devil as a hideous fanged, winged creature, as terrifying and awful as anything science fiction has yet to conjure up.

These artistic creations reveal something far more important about the nature of angels than their appearance (about which they really reveal very little). Their expressions, their posture, the tasks they perform offer us visual representations of what we do know about their behavior as leaders, messengers, spirits, powerful and majestic beings, and as protectors, healers, comforters, and champions. These are the features on which we should concentrate as we consider turning to them to serve as models for our own attitudes and behavior.

The idea of angels as models for us to learn from and strive to emulate is as old as the concept of angels themselves. We would do well to emulate them, seeking to develop their strengths and virtues in our lives, especially, as I will point out later, since these qualities can only enhance our physical and mental health and our enjoyment of all that is about us here on earth.

IV

A Physician Looks at Angels

In which you will learn why a doctor would be concerned with angels at all

ONE DAY a few weeks ago I stopped by my bank to make a deposit. I was the only customer at the time. As we usually do, the teller and I exchanged pleasantries as she was stamping the checks and handing me back my pink deposit slips. She asked me whether I was working on a new book. "Yes," I replied. "I'm writing one about angels." She looked positively ecstatic and, turning to the teller next to her, said excitedly, "The doctor is writing about angels." The other woman smiled broadly and said, "That's wonderful. I love angels."

A few days later I had to go back to the bank again, this time to speak with the manager. After we had concluded our business, she took me aside and asked me if it was true that I was writing about angels. I said it was. "I believe in angels," she said. "But I wouldn't have expected *you* to be writing about them. I mean. . .you're a. . ." I finished her sentence for her: "A psychiatrist," I said. She blushed. "I understand where you're coming from," I said. "Psychiatrists aren't known for believing in God or angels. But some do, and I guess I'm one of them."

She then proceeded to tell me that she believed she had had an encounter with an angel. "I haven't spoken about this in years. When I was sixteen, I nearly drowned. I was swimming off Jones Beach. The waves got really big. I was terrified. I shouted to my friends on the beach. I could see them running around and waving at me. But I was too far out, and it was too rough for them to swim to get me. All they could do was find the lifeguard and get him to come out after me. I went under once. I came up again, and then went under a second time. I knew I was going to drown. All of a sudden, I felt two powerful hands behind me, grabbing me by my shoulders. It had to be a man. He pulled me rapidly toward the beach, and he only let go of me when my feet could touch bottom and I could stand by myself. I looked around. There was no one there. By then, two of my friends were already in the surf, coming to help me ashore. "Where is the man who saved me?" I asked them. They shook their heads. They hadn't seen anyone with me. I had been brought back to shallow water before the lifeguard could even reach me. I have to believe it was an angel, and I'll never forget what he did for me."

After my conversation with her, however, I began to appreciate the fact that there would be others, too, who would react with surprise to learn that a physician—a psychiatrist, no less—had chosen to write a book that involved angels, even though my primary focus was about human beings learning something from qualities attributed to angels that they might find valuable in their own very real, very visible lives here on earth.

Certainly you won't find angels referred to in medical literature or in Freud. I can't recall angels ever being talked about in the hospital dining room when we doctors would get together and chat over lunch. An exception might be the use of the word "angel" to describe a nurse who was unusually dedicated to her job of caring for the sick. Of course, a few of my colleagues who were interested in theatrical productions would use the term "angel" to mean the person who puts up the money to back a play.

But as a rule, doctors don't give the matter of angels much serious thought, if any thought at all. Yet they witness throughout their careers numerous remarkable events, such as moments of diagnostic inspiration, or totally unexpected recoveries from the brink of death.

One physician, whose studies may have involved angels, is Dr. Raymond A. Moody. In his book about near-death experiences, *Life After Life*, Dr. Moody reported that the most common description of near-death experiences is an encounter with a light of unearthly brilliance. "Not one person has expressed any doubt whatsoever that it was a being, a being of light... The love and warmth which emanate from this being to the dying person are utterly beyond words," he goes on, "and he feels completely surrounded by it and taken up in it, completely at ease in the presence of this being."

Some people may dismiss these perceptions as a product of faulty brain metabolism. But one could also interpret them as evidence of angels simply going about their routine business.

Maybe we scientists can't prove there are angels. But we can't prove there aren't, either. There is still a great deal about the universe that we do not understand. All we have to do to appreciate this fact is to compare what the practice of medicine was like a hundred years ago and what it is like today: antibiotics, antidepressants, drugs to relieve hypertension and diabetes and a host of other once disabling and fatal diseases. It's not good science to believe that what we have no evidence for today cannot become an established fact tomorrow. An open mind and healthy curiosity are prerequisites for scientific inquiry. And if the nature of angels is not a subject worthy of both, what is?

Doctors should be aware of angels, or at least be aware that many people do believe in them, and respect their patients' beliefs. Moreover, a person's spirituality can have a great deal of influence on his or her physical and mental health. Slowly but surely, medicine is beginning to appreciate and study these effects.

In a recent issue of the *American Journal of Psychiatry*, Dr. Harold G. Koenig and his colleagues reported on a research program that demonstrated that among medically ill older patients suffering with clinical depression, those who had a greater degree of *intrinsic religious faith* recovered much more quickly than those who did not. Reviewing other studies reported in the scientific literature, they also pointed out that a substantial number of patients use religious belief or activity to cope with the stress of physical illness, and that such patients appear to be less depressed than those who do not or can not rely on faith. "Although the exact mechanism is uncertain, religious beliefs may provide a world view in which medical illness, suffering, and death can be better understood and accepted. Alternatively, they may provide a basis for self-esteem that is more resilient than sources [of self-esteem] that decline with increasing age and worsening health."

Other studies have verified the powerful effect of prayer on recovery from physical illness. Many of us have heard of such miracles. A friend of mine, a highly educated and urbane woman in her seventies, was recently diagnosed as having bladder cancer. Within a couple of weeks, her grandson was diagnosed as having a brain tumor. Both were seen in excellent medical centers. As it happened, her late husband's son was a minister living in a medium-sized community in Oregon. Hearing the news, he initiated a massive prayer effort among his own congregation as well as those of the other churches in town. When my friend returned to her doctors for a final checkup before surgery, they could find no evidence of her cancer. And when her grandson was reexamined for his brain tumor, the doctors couldn't find that either.

The spirituality of a patient and a patient's family and friends is a vital element in recovery from illness and in the phenomenon of healing. It's a power with which physicians should want to ally themselves as they carry out their own efforts to diagnose and cure. In the case of psychiatry, or any profession that attends to the mind, the spirit dare not be ignored.

In *Modern Man in Search of a Soul*, Carl Jung wrote: "However far-fetched it may sound [at a time when atheist Sigmund Freud dominated the psychoanalytic scene], experience shows that many neuroses are caused by the fact that people blind themselves to their own religious promptings because of a childish passion for rational enlightenment. The psychologist of today ought to realize once and for all that we are no longer dealing with questions of dogma and creed. A religious attitude is an element in psychic life whose importance can hardly be overrated. And it is precisely for the religious outlook that the sense of historical continuity is indispensable."

When you consider what doctors are expected to do and what angels are described as doing, the similarities become apparent. Angels are communicators. The practice of medicine depends on successful communication between doctors and their patients. Failure in this area is at the heart of many a poor outcome. Nowhere is that more apparent than in psychiatry, where communication is as important a tool of treatment as fine instruments are to a surgeon removing a neoplasm of the kidney or a clot in the artery of a patient's heart. We have to listen carefully to what patients say—as well as to what they communicate nonverbally. We have to inquire about important events in patients' lives and about their reactions to those events. We have to know what to tell them, and when and how to most effectively present them with new insights into themselves.

Angels and doctors are both healers—although angels may have the advantage of performing a miracle here and there, while we doctors must depend on more ordinary methods of diagnosis and treatment. We are both expected to empathize with our patients, to truly understand what they are experiencing, and to inspire hope. And while we often must work hard to develop proficiency at comforting and reassuring our patients, it's second nature for the angels.

Professionals who help patients with their psychological difficulties—psychiatrists, psychologists, social workers, counselors—regularly teach and encourage those we counsel to emulate angels, even though I'm sure most therapists don't think of it that way at all. Take generosity, for example. When I was a psychiatric resident in training, I had a teacher who would make rounds with me every week, visiting all the patients under my care, spending at least ten minutes with them, and later discussing the cases with me in the privacy of his office. Invariably, at one time or another, he would ask this question of the patients: "How much do you give of yourself to other people?" He seemed to assume I understood why. I didn't. So finally I asked him, "Why?" "Because giving of yourself to others is an important part of being mentally healthy," he said. "Cultivating a generosity of spirit can help many patients to recover, or at least to do a lot better than they have been doing. If you're not generous, you isolate yourself. You're alone, and lonely. You can become more and more preoccupied with your own needs, a self-centeredness that can easily turn into selfishness. And, of course, selfishness destroys relationships that are so essential to anybody's mental and physical health, to say nothing of one's happiness." In the forty years since I was given that lesson, I have seen the truth of it confirmed in any number of situations, professionally and in my own personal life as well.

I believe that angels possess free will, and so do we. Webster's dictionary defines will as "the power of making a reasoned choice or decision or of controlling one's own actions." Isn't that what we're continually trying to get our patients to do?—getting the patient who's afraid of flying in planes to fly, or the one who's afraid of crowded place to go into department stores—to break out of their prisons of fear? Aren't we working to free them from the bondage of their pasts, to help them let go of old hurts and resentments so that they can be in charge of their lives in the present? Even Freud, who considered God, and I'm sure angels too, as so much nonsense, suggested that the purpose of psychoanalysis was to achieve of new balance among a person's ego (where options are understood and choices made), superego (where we define what we expect of ourselves, and where our sense of right and wrong resides), and id (that hotbed of animal passions). "Where id was, ego shall be," he proposed. In other words, he unwittingly suggested that one of the objectives of the form of treatment he originated was to make its recipients more like angels.

So there are plenty of reasons why physicians in general, and psychiatrists and other professional therapists in particular, should take the time to notice angels. After all, emulating their most remarkable qualities can only help us all achieve fuller, healthier, happier lives.

The Seven
Remarkable
Strengths
of Angels

V

The Seven
Remarkable Strengths
of Angels

In which you will find out the special gifts that angels possess and that you can emulate in your efforts to become a better, more effective person

WE KNOW a good deal about what angels are like and what they do from their appearances in the Hebrew Scriptures and the New Testament, as well as angel encounters that others have related. A number of threads run throughout all angel accounts. Angels— good angels, that is—are loving and respectful. They are holy. They encourage those they visit toward goodness and protect them from harm. They are communicators par excellence. They are rescuers and leaders and guides. They are healers. They are wonderful singers. They can travel from one location to another faster than the speed of light. They are powerful, yet humble.

They are unbelievably successful. Well, not all of them. Remember those who fell from grace.

So why choose only seven of their marvelous gifts? Seven is a special number. God is said to have created the world in seven days. There are believed to be seven angels before the throne of God. "Seventh heaven" was considered the home of God on his divine throne, along with the highest orders of angels, the seraphim, cherubim, and thrones. It derives from the tradition of seven heavens, a concept that came from the notion of seven "levels of reality," which, in turn, evolved in human thinking at a time when the earth was thought to be the center of the universe, surrounded by the five then-known planets, the moon, and the sun. Seven is also the number of angels in the highest order of angels. Hebrew scriptures (Tobit 12:15, Daniel 10:13, Zechariah 4:10) refers to seven holy angels who present the prayers of the saints and enter into the presence of the glory of the Holy One.

Then too there are the seven deadly sins—pride, envy, lust, gluttony, sloth, anger, and greed—against which we must struggle throughout our lives, and to prevail, we can use every bit of angel strength we can muster.

Traditional Christianity holds that there are seven sacraments to enrich our spirituality: baptism, confirmation, the Eucharist, matrimony, penance (confessing one's sins), extreme unction, and holy orders.

Seven is also a lucky number, or so it's said. And it can be found in the title of a number of successful books, such as The Seven Pillars of Wisdom T. E. Lawrence (of Arabia) and Stephen Covey's Seven Habits of Highly Effective People. Research has suggested that seven may be the ideal number of people to make up an effective group, whether in group therapy, a team of scientists, or creative people working to develop new products or new marketing strategies. Seven's a big enough number to be significant and a small enough one to be comprehensible. From a practical point of view, selecting seven of the angels' strongest traits and suggesting that we all would do well to understand and practice these, modeling ourselves after these unique beings, offers us a limited set of qualities that we can focus on, and gradually master, without being overwhelmed by the effort.

These seven admirable attributes are *free will, the power of knowing, love, the art of communicating, the mission to guide and protect, the ability to heal*, and, of course, *spirituality*.

We do not have to look far to recognize them in the angels, and, to a lesser degree, in ourselves.

1. **Free Will**. The most dramatic illustration of the freedom that God gave the angels is Lucifer's rebellion, which ended in his exile and that of his followers.

2. **Knowing**. When asked what angels do all day long, Peter Kreeft, Professor of Philosophy at Boston College, in *Angels (and Demons)*, answers: "Have insights. Insights just keep popping into their minds, a never-ending stream. They are like super scientists, artists, poets, and philosophers. Angels are intuitive intelligences. They 'just know' and contemplate what they know: God, themselves, each other, and us."

3. **Love.** Angels are true altruists. They wish everyone well—each other—and all of us whom they guard and protect. Their every action, whether saving

someone from freezing to death or comforting a grief-stricken child or leading Joseph, Mary, and Jesus to Egypt to escape the wrath of Herod, attests to their enormous love.

4. **Marvelous abilities to communicate.** Angels inspire us, stimulating our imaginations and giving us invaluable insights. In Luke 1:26–38, the angel Gabriel, delivering God's message to Mary, says reassuringly, succinctly: "Greetings, you who are highly favored! The Lord is with you. Do not be afraid, Mary, you have found favor with God. You will be with child and give birth to a son, and you are to give him the name Jesus."

5. **A mission to guard and protect.** Each of us is lucky enough to have a guardian angel assigned to us from the day we are born. Joan Webster Anderson, in her book *Where Angels Walk*, tells of her son Tim's plight when he and a friend were stranded in their broken-down automobile on a rural access road to the Indiana tollway on a bitterly cold and snowy night. They faced freezing to death. Tim prayed. Barely able to stay awake, they suddenly saw the lights of another car. It was a tow truck. The driver attached chains to their car and pulled it back to a friend's home in Fort Wayne. Although their friend, Don, came out quickly to greet them, he saw no tow-truck. There were no tire tracks in the snow other than those from Tim's own car. Tim was given no bill for services, not even a goodbye.

St. Paul, under arrest, was being transported by sea to Italy when a tremendous storm arose, threatening to sink the ship and drown all aboard. "I urge you now to take heart," says Paul, "for there will be no loss of life among you. . .For last night, there stood by me an angel of the Lord to whom I belong and whom I worship, and he said: 'Do not be afraid, Paul. You must stand before Caesar; and so God has granted safety to you and to all those who are sailing with you.'" (Acts 27: 23–24)

6. **The Power to Heal and Console.** In Luke 22:42–43, in his agony in the Garden of Gethsemane, Christ cries out: "Father, if you are willing, take this cup from me; still not my will, but yours be done. Then there appeared to him an angel from heaven, strengthening him."

   In Tobit 12:14–18, the angel Raphael instructs Tobias to apply fish gall to the eyes of his father, who is blind. Tibia's eyesight is restored, and Raphael says, "God sent me to heal you."

7. **Spirituality**. It is here that the nature of angels and our nature assume remarkable similarity. Angels aren't humans without bodies, however. They are a different breed of being. But our spirits share their immortality, as well as the power to think and the power to choose. It is this spiritual quality that gives us the strength to believe in God (whom angels know and hence do not have to have faith), and to pray with sincerity and perseverance, and to transcend this material world and find greater meaning to our existence.

Now let's proceed to examine each of these wonderful gifts in greater detail, and see how we might strengthen them in our own lives.

In each of our lives, there are usually several points at which, because we have achieved a singular level of success or, more often, have been brought to our knees by a defeat that humiliates, we are uniquely positioned to make choices that will determine the course of the rest of our lives. At such time, we feel a heady kind of freedom born of accomplishment, or, conversely, the kind of freedom that comes from the hopelessness of having nothing left of what we once valued. It is at these points that we must be ready to make a right choice.

What comes before is a period of getting ready. What comes afterward depends upon how ready we are and what choices we make.

Putting the Pieces Together Again
FREDERIC FLACH, MD

VI

THE FIRST STRENGTH
The Freedom to Choose

In which you will learn how to make better choices and to have more control over the direction and quality of your life

*T*HIS IS where it all begins. You chose to read this book. You chose to think about the special powers of angels. You will choose whether or not you wish to develop these in yourself. If you've come this far and you decide that love and generosity of spirit and knowing and healing and guiding and protecting and spirituality aren't for you, you can put this book down and find something else to do with your time. But if you want to go forward, it's time to take a closer look at angel will, and how valuable a gift we have also been given, to be free to determine the course of our own lives here on earth.

Angel will is unencumbered by all the physical urges and distractions that our bodies throw into the mix. It's hard to imagine what kind of choices angels really have to make on a day-to-day basis. Of course, we're all familiar with the big choice, when Lucifer and his followers chose to defy God himself—Revelation 12:79 says that "war broke out in heaven. Michael and his angels fought against the dragon. The dragon and his angels fought back, but they were defeated and there was no longer any place for them in heaven." I suppose that there may have been moments when God himself has regretted endowing angels (and us humans) with free will, considering the serious mischief we have all chosen to pursue. It can't be pleasant knowing that any of your creations could be so ungrateful and would have to suffer eternally for their abhorrent behavior. At the same time, angels and people make so many wonderful choices that perhaps these make up for it in the end.

On a more mundane level, it's difficult to imagine an angel refusing when God gives him some assignment, like delivering a message to a sleeping mother, waking her up, and urging her to check on her small son who needs to be taken to the hospital to have his suddenly inflamed appendix removed. Could you imagine an angel saying, "Sorry, I'm busy practicing with the choir. I'll take care of it tomorrow?"

Angels have been given a broad mandate to guard and protect us. How they do that may be left up to them. They may decide whether to deliver you a message via your dreams or don the costume of a human being—a fireman's uniform, for example—and rescue you from a burning building. But even with their responsibilities clearly defined, they still have the freedom to live up to them or not.

How free is free?

Human freedom is a complicated business. We have been endowed with free will, just like the angels. But, unlike that of angels, the extent of our freedom is affected by a great many variables. How we use our free will takes many forms. Exercising it involves working both with *and* against our physical nature. Our freedom is always restricted to some degree, by external forces, by laws and social customs, by organizational rules and personal resources, and by the people all around us who also have their free wills in play. You may want to drive an automobile, but you shouldn't because you haven't yet been able to pass the driver's test to obtain your license. You may want to spend a week in Florida, assuming you don't live there already, but you can't afford to right now. You may want to improve your conflict-riddled relationship with your husband or wife, but he or she is unwilling to make any move in that direction, perhaps out of hopelessness or because of old hurts and resentments that refuse to go away.

Our freedom is also curtailed by our own inner limitations. You can feel so discouraged that a sense of futility weakens your resolution. Or fatigue may produce inertia. Or ignorance may stand in your way. Or maybe you haven't grown used to making up your own mind and have grown too dependent on doing the will of others.

Degrees of freedom

Looking back over a lifetime, I can see a number of significant turning points when I made choices that proved to have a profound influence on the rest of my life. To each of these choices I have given a rough score, indicating how much freedom I believe I actually enjoyed at the time. For example, my decision to enter medical school could be considered about 70 percent free. Becoming a doctor was something my parents wanted me to consider seriously, and I did. Even though I flirted with other career directions, I was far from a rebellious young man. I couldn't see myself writing the great American novel after years of bouncing around the world as a sailor on a freighter; or serving drinks in a sleazy bar in Dayton, Ohio; or parking cars at the Brown Derby, hoping to get a screen test. Sure, I dreamed of being a writer, even an actor, or of owning a radio station and newspaper. I thought of being a foreign corespondent, like Edward R. Murrow, or going to Wall Street and making a great fortune and becoming a philanthropist, like Rockefeller—not that nature had given me the passion for wealth and the basic toughness that such success would require!

Medicine had a strong appeal in itself. Being a doctor was prestigious and economically rewarding. It promised a respected position in society. It afforded me the sense that every day of every year I could get up in the morning knowing that I would be doing something I considered worth doing: helping people. I applied to Johns Hopkins, Harvard, and Cornell University Medical College. Still, I wasn't entirely sure of my decision. So I thought that if I weren't accepted by any of these three, I might choose a different career to pursue.

The very day I visited Cornell, as soon as my interviews were done the dean asked me whether, if he agreed to take me, I would agree to attend. I said yes.

He then signed and handed me a letter of acceptance—a most unusual thing, even in those days. I never looked back.

That's why I say that my choice to become a physician was about 70 percent a free one. It seems to me that something else was at work at that pivotal turning point in my life, moving things around like a stage director in the theater, so that I would end up where I find myself at this point in time, if I cooperated.

How free were your choices? Were you any clearer about what you wanted to do with your life than I was? Did you decide to go to college? Which one did you choose? How confident were you when it came to selecting your major? Did you head for graduate school, knowing what profession or career you wanted to pursue, or did you, like most people, simply flounder, taking your first job because it was offered to you, hoping for a light to go on in your head a little later on?

And what about getting married? Did you date someone for several years, get to know each other pretty well, and decide (with a freedom level of about 90 percent) to make the commitments? Or were you swept off your feet with passion and romance, rapidly becoming deeply involved with each other, marry in a couple of months (with a freedom level of about 35 percent) and spend a few years together in a state of mutual disillusionment before getting divorced?

And what about divorce, or breaking up any close relationship? How much freedom did you have available to you then? Was this a choice you made a hundred times in your mind before finally coming to terms with a no-win situation? Did you have to overcome fear—fear of being without that other person, fear of being

alone? Was your freedom compromised by embarrassment, or a sense of defeat, or a demoralization that
resulted from the inherent destructiveness of the relationship in which you had found yourself trapped? Or
was your decision impulsive, poorly thought through,
motivated more by anger of the moment than reasonable appraisal, in which your freedom quotient might
be as low as, shall we say, 15 percent?

The fact that our minds and spirits are locked within our bodies frequently makes the exercise of our free
will problematic. But that shouldn't stop us from appreciating the power of will that we possess and practicing
ways to increase our freedom quotient and improve the
quality of the decisions we do make.

BEGIN WITH SMALL CHOICES, THEN MOVE ON TO THE BIGGER ONES

You can start with small choices. When very little is at
stake, your emotions aren't so likely to cloud your
vision. They should be the easiest to make. For
instance, you may be planning to celebrate the birthday
of a member of your family or a close friend by taking
him or her out to dinner. What restaurant will you
select? Thoughtfulness, another angel trait, will encourage you to choose the kind of restaurant that your birthday celebrant will enjoy. This means that you must
know—knowing is another angel strength—your
friend's tastes and preferences. But if you don't, you
could ask and let him or her help you make the choice.

Or perhaps you plan to take a vacation. You look
through the travel section of your newspaper. You drop

by a travel agency and get a few brochures. You know some of the places where you'd like to go, but perhaps you have neither the time nor the money to trek in Nepal, or go on safari in Kenya, or sail around the Cape of Good Hope. For the moment, you have to make a more modest choice. So you decide on the Canadian ocean provinces, Nova Scotia, New Brunswick, and Prince Edward Island. You get out your calendar and check dates. You call the airlines and get the best fares they offer. You book some of your hotels, while other stopovers you leave to chance.

Now, these examples may seem awfully trite—who can't decide where to take a friend for dinner or what kind of vacation to plan? The fact is, I've had trouble making decisions as simple as these, and these are no-brainers, as they say. It's not likely that much emotion will come into play, such as fear (unless you're afraid to fly) or loneliness (in which you may not want to go anywhere by yourself) or mixed feelings about your friend (as when something he or she did or said that hurt your feelings conflicts with your wish to show him or her a good time). Emotions such as these can reduce your freedom quotient, interfering with your ability to think and choose freely, so that you may end up feeling unsure or frustrated as you go over and over your options, procrastinating (a bad habit, not characteristic of angels), maybe putting a decision off indefinitely.

I knew a young woman once who never bought her boyfriend a present—not for Christmas; not for his birthday. It wasn't that she didn't love him. Nor was she basically ungenerous. But she was perfectionistic. "He's so wonderful," she told me, "I can't think of anything good enough for him." She was also afraid of rejection.

"I don't want him to be disappointed." I suggested that she was probably a chronic disappointment to him on this count, and encouraged her to use her will power and make the effort to find a gift for him the next time an occasion presented itself. "You know him well enough to find something he'd like. I can't believe you don't. Do it, and get into the habit of doing it. It takes a little practice, that's all."

Practice will help prepare you for the larger choices in life. The need to make some of these choices is more or less predictable: how far you'll go in school, what kind of work you'll do, when and whom you will marry, whether you'll have children and how many, whether you'll stay married or end up divorced, whether or not you'll lead a physically, mentally, and spiritually healthy life. The need to make other kinds of choices, such as how to handle your life after being disabled in an automobile crash, being widowed at forty, or losing a child, cannot be predicted. In either case, the quality of your decisions will be enhanced by everything you do to strengthen your gift of free will.

CHOICES THAT TEST OUR MORAL FIBER

In our efforts to emulate the angels, we must practice acts of will. And it's in the small things that we can hone our strength and ready ourselves for the big choices that can make or break us, especially those that test our moral fiber. It's the small lie that makes it easier to tell the big lie. It's the small demonstration of courage, like making a telephone call you've been dreading, perhaps to a friend who hasn't called you in a long time and whom you think may have forgotten you, that sets the stage for overcoming fear. Resisting small temptations can help you resist the big temptation, as when the opportunity to have an affair is handed to you in a most appealing way and you turn it down because of your faithfulness to a love for someone else.

Most of us are not going to face the decision of whether to engage in great moral evils, like murder. Our moral crises will be more mundane, but they are no less moments when we are asked to choose between what we deem to be right and what we know is wrong. I'm assuming that you aren't one of those criminal types for whom right and wrong have no meaning. You'd hardly be reading a book about angels if you were!

I have a trainer to supervise my weight-lifting exercises. When I first walked into his gym, I noticed a plaque on the wall of his office containing the ten commandments. I was surprised. I hadn't read them in a long time. Honor God. Honor our parents. Don't commit adultery. Don't steal anyone's worldly goods, or spouses, much less their lives. Not a difficult set of precepts to understand or remember. They were designed specifically for us humans, who are vulnerable to sins of the flesh.

If we run down these commandments in our minds, we will immediately see what most of the situations are in which we will have the opportunity to use our free will, to choose among what's good, what's not so good, and what's positively evil. As I mentioned, we won't often have the opportunity, let alone the desire, to commit premeditated murder. *But there are many ways to commit murder slowly, over years, starving someone of love, destroying a person's self-respect with caustic and den-*

igrating words, behaving abusively toward helpless children or helpless elders.

How much do we choose to respect and care for elderly parents? How much everyday love do we choose to show the people with whom we live and work? How much loyalty do we choose to give our friends? How much reverence do we choose to give God?

It's sometimes hard to avoid coveting your neighbor's goods, especially when you see your neighbors making millions of dollars (even billions), building gargantuan houses, driving luxury cars, and taking exotic vacations. You can choose to ignore them and go on about your business, which may be the only thing you can do. You can choose to sneak out at night and write nasty words on their garages, which could land you in jail. You can choose to go out and try to make your own millions, so you can build your own house right next to theirs. You can choose to join an environmental protection group and work to save what seashore still remains pristine and intact. You can choose to concentrate on enjoying the blessings of your own life, because you already have what you truly value, and you feel reasonably comfortable that the future will take care of itself, with God's help. The choice is yours.

The choice is always yours. And it's not always easy. You go to a cocktail reception at a convention you're attending. A pretty woman or a handsome man makes advances to you. You go along with it, or you don't. Or you discover a piece of unpleasant information about someone you know—the IRS is investigating him for not paying his taxes, or she had her Visa card canceled because she was too far behind in her payments—and keep it to yourself or spread the word. It's your call.

EXERCISING YOUR FREE WILL

How did I exercise my free will within the last twenty-four hours? Yesterday afternoon I decided to telephone one of my patients who had recently been discharged from the hospital following hip replacement surgery. I also contacted her own physician to get an update on her medical status. You could say that's what I should have done. It is. But some other doctors might have put it off until today, or tomorrow, or the day after that, out of laziness, or because they felt they were just too occupied to find five minutes for a phone call, or they'd rather take the day off to play golf. Doctors don't always do what they ought to. Nobody does.

I decided to take two of my winter jackets to the cleaners. I'd been putting that off for weeks. Having an hour free after lunch, I chose to go to Barnes and Noble to buy one of my sons a copy of Patrick O'Brian's *The Yellow Admiral* for Christmas, even though Christmas was still five months away. I also decided to write a note to the widow of an old friend of mine to see how she was doing, and to turn down an invitation to be on a panel at a medical conference in the fall because I had too many other obligations to fulfill. Ordinary choices on an ordinary day.

The last big decision I made was moving to a new office from one I'd occupied for nearly thirty years. It was a tough one. I knew it was something I should do, and in fact it's worked out very well. But to me it represented a profound emotional loss, and many's the night I lay awake, painfully going over the pros and cons again and again in my mind.

Of course, I don't necessarily choose well. I've made my share of bad choices, just as everyone else has. I won't mention any of the not-so-great stocks I've purchased from time to time.

We have to exercise our freedom the same way that we exercise our bodies. That's the only way to make free will a habit. The choices we make should be based on a set of standards that do us proud. Some decisions will require more research and contemplation than others. Sometimes, in fact, we will choose not to choose.

Our free will can only be exercised within the limitations of our knowledge and our emotions. We may not be able to say yes or no right away. We may intentionally postpone a decision until we find a crucial piece of information or a moment of illumination and clarity that will increase our chances of making a right decision. Buying a home is one of the biggest decisions most people in this country have to make. I know one couple who knew that they wanted to live in a particular town. So they went to a realtor and asked for a computer printout of all the properties on the market as well as those that had been sold during the prior three-year period. The realtor was surprised by their request, but obliged. List in hand, they drove around looking at a number of these houses to get a clearer idea of what they liked and didn't like and what they might be able to get for what they could afford. Eventually they narrowed their choice to three homes. They examined each one carefully. Then they made an offer on the one they subsequently purchased. Good choices are often preceded by solid homework.

READINESS IS ALL

But there will be times when you simply don't know what to choose. Something easy, for example a dress for a dance. Or something pretty serious, such as whether to change jobs or commit yourself in a relationship or terminate one that's gone sour. This is where faith and optimism come in. Free will does not mean that any of us can control every aspect of our lives. Far from it. Many of the most important things that happen to us may appear to have happened by pure chance.

You may well ask, How can I be the captain of my fate when there seem to be so many variables shaping the direction of my life? This is where two philosophies of freedom appear to collide. Antoine de Saint-Exupéry, a French writer, an adventurer, a World War II pilot, and an idealist, wrote in *Flight to Arras*, "The real task is to succeed in setting man free by making him master of himself."

On the other hand, philosopher Alan Watts, in his book *The Watercourse Way*, offered a more Eastern viewpoint. He wrote, "People try to force issues only when realizing that it can't be done." He argued that we should allow events to emerge and realize that the course our lives will take is partly determined by a blueprint of every person's destiny as the background against which all important choices are to be made—a time and place for everything; a readiness for things to happen. And when the time and place are not now, when we are not ready or our world is not ready, we may simply have to wait as things beyond our control fall into place. This kind of waiting can truly test our ability to hope and to believe.

A young man I know in his middle thirties wants very much to meet a woman, be in love, marry, and have a family. But there is no one on the horizon. He had had two previous relationships, each lasting for several years. I knew the women. Had he married either of them, he would surely have been embroiled in a very hazardous relationship, or been long since divorced, perhaps paying alimony the rest of his life, and having children who would have suffered either way. When we speak of his situation, I remind him how lucky he is that his choices (he almost married each, guided by a distortion of who and what they were) had been thwarted by circumstance (a guardian angel at work?). Now he was free, unencumbered, and more ready than he had ever been before to meet someone with whom he could share a commitment. He has found this perspective very reassuring. He knows it is true. He can choose to go out and meet people, which he does, and keep an open mind and heart. But beyond that he must rely on the watercourse way, with the help of angels, to bring him safely to a point at which he can make a free and considered choice.

What was the line in the movie *Field of Dreams*? "If you build it, they will come." There were angels in this film, as I recall.

Readiness is all—inner readiness; readiness in the world about us. It is at this point, I believe, that we can exert our free will with the greatest freedom and hope to achieve the very best results. My older son, Christopher, dated a young woman, Martha, for several years. They both wanted to marry, but Chris didn't feel ready. He was still working on his Ph.D. in psychology. He wanted to be more established before taking on the responsibilities of marriage. So they went their separate ways. He moved from New York to a small town in North Carolina, where he did his internship in clinical psychology. While he was there, he did not meet any other woman whom he cared for in a serious way. One warm spring day, a year and a half later, he came to visit me in New York. He was walking down Park Avenue when he unexpectedly ran into Martha. She asked him one question: "Are you ready?" He knew what she meant. A few months later they were married, and now they are both successful in their careers and their marriage, and they live in San Francisco with my seven-year-old grandson, Malcolm.

"Readiness is all" is a line from Shakespeare's play *Hamlet*. If you haven't seen the video of Kenneth Branagh's production of *Hamlet*, you really should choose to see it. The nice thing about video is that you don't have to watch it all at once (This movie runs nearly four hours, and that's a long time to sit in a theater.) Moreover, you can rewind it to watch your favorite scenes as often as you wish. I did. One such scene occurs near the end of the play. Hamlet is about to fight the duel with Laertes in which he will die. He is speaking to his dear friend Horatio:

"If it be now, 'tis not to come; if it be not to come, it will be now; if it be not now, yet it will come: *the readiness is all*."   [emphasis added]

Inner readiness and the readiness of circumstance create the best environment for us to exercise our free wills. They involve putting ourselves in the right places (although we may not know how right they are at first), at the right times (timing is everything). This means we must reach out to the world, being there, doing, so that things can happen when they're meant to. It means being patient, not making impulsive and often stupid choices out of frustration. It certainly means staying open to inspiration, whether sudden insights come from our own imaginations, or are placed there by an angel. It requires an affirmative approach to life, hopeful rather than gloomy expectations (not to be confused with entitlement), optimism rather than pessimism. It calls for faith that our choices will place us firmly on the path that God wants us to follow.

We cannot control what is beyond us. But we can prepare ourselves. How, then, beyond making ourselves available to the future, can we be ready?

PREPARATION FOR CHOICES

It begins with knowledge (an angel strength) of ourselves, of others, of the world we live in. Not just limited to what we learn from our parents and in school, or from books, or from watching television. Not only what we learn by being taught, and then, by trial and error, master—such as how to ride a bike, or ice-skate, or drive an automobile, or cook, or build a cabinet, or repair a leaky faucet. Nor just what we learn by listening to what people say. It involves *all* that we experience; it requires us to look into ourselves for understanding and to pay attention to our dreams and to something that is both the blessing and the bane of our human nature, called emotions.

Educating ourselves about the nature of emotions is essential in the cultivation of our freedom. When my children were little, we used to recite a short rhyme about feelings. It may sound familiar to many of you. It went this way:

> When you're happy and you know it, clap your hands,
> When you're sad and you know it, go boo-hoo, boo-hoo
> When you're mad and you know it, stamp your feet.

You have no idea how many grownups don't know what they feel from one moment to the next or get mixed up with regard to the true nature of their emotions. They feel irritable and angry when they're really depressed, or they think they're very much in love when sexual passion is all that's in play, or they feel brave and behave in foolhardy ways when they really ought to be terrified. We can all benefit by learning more about emotions and how they affect our judgment and our choices.

Feelings can get in the way of freedom. But they're freedom's fuel as well. It's part of the human condition. It's joy that motivates us to love, for example, and love that makes us feel joyous. Tears of sadness move us to empathic moments. Tears of anger motivate us to take righteous action.

Materialistic and deterministic philosophies can get in our way too. Freedom is a power we share with the angels. To protect our power, we must be prepared to reject philosophies that would have us believe that we are little more than victims of fate, products of our environments, and that social forces and/or subconscious sexual and violent instincts lie at the heart of everything we think and do.

PRACTICE WON'T MAKE US PERFECT, BUT IT WILL HELP US COME A BIT CLOSER TO IT

We must practice making choices. Consider the choices you can make today. I will go shopping for groceries. I will finish off that report for the boss. I will call up a friend. I will read the newspaper and keep up with what's happening in the world. I will rent a video and watch a movie tonight. I will tell at least one person I love how much I love him or her. I will say a prayer.

Practice using your free will to improve yourself, to help those around you to grow, to *reject what's evil and to embrace what's genuinely good.*

The late Lawrence Kubie, a renowned psychoanalyst, defined *will power* for me as "the energy required to overcome a phobia." What he meant was that you had to use all your strength of will to go against the fear that phobias contain, for instance forcing yourself to leave the house or go into a crowded department store when either of these is a nightmare for you. I could identify with that—not that I suffered with phobias. But I can recall forcing myself to do certain things when I didn't feel like it, such as homework or chores around the house when I was growing up. If you haven't exercised your free will in quite a while, you may have to go through some pain as you start doing so—exercise trainers call it "burning" as you use your muscles to lift heavier and heavier weights. But the wonderful part of this practice is that as you perfect your free will, you will find yourself doing more and more and more, making better choices, and achieving your goals with much less effort and a great deal of spontaneity. *Spontaneous will is what angel freedom is all about.*

So don't dillydally with your life. Don't drift along, avoiding commitments you would do well to make, letting love pass you by, ignoring your career, until too many doors have shut tight against you, as doors have a way of doing. Make two lists, things to be decided upon and done right now, and things that can and possibly should wait, and live by your list. Pretty soon you'll find that you have made the exercise of your free will a habit to be proud of, and you'll be well on your way to becoming the successful and happy person you always wanted to be.

GUIDELINES FOR MODELING OURSELVES AFTER ANGELS

Making Choices

- Choose to become more angel-like in your behavior.

- Practice making small choices. Don't just go through the day mindlessly. Even if the things you do are not very different from one day to the next, do them with conscious decision from time to time. I choose to work on this report. I choose to prepare dinner. I choose to call up my friend and make plans for next weekend. Such an exercise will remind you of your freedom and strengthen your sense of determination when larger issues arise.

- Be well prepared, especially when it comes to making big decisions. Gather all the information you need. If you're thinking of getting married, be sure you know each other well enough. If you're thinking of defining or changing the direction of your career, be sure you know what your talents—and shortcomings—are, and the opportunities that exist for you to pursue these. If you're considering retirement, be sure your financial house is in order (hopefully, you've made choices about this years ago, for example setting up a retirement plan); and if you plan to move, become familiar with the place where you intend to go before you buy a house or rent an apartment and wake up one morning full of regret.

- Keep an eye on your emotions, which may entice you to make rash and impulsive choices out of fear, anger, or unwarranted enthusiasm. This way, you'll maximize your freedom quotient, the amount of freedom available to you in making your choices.

- Be patient. Know when it's not the right time to make some important decision. When you don't know what decision to make, use your creativity to explore all the options and consider their consequences. Simmer. Let your subconscious do some of the sorting of ideas, until you come up with one or more that really seem right.

- Don't expect all your choices to be good choices. You'll make mistakes. Rather than brood over them, examine them, learn from them so as to improve the quality of your decisions the next time around.

- Remember: Readiness is all. Most of the major choices that we make depend upon an inner readiness *and* the readiness of the world around us. It's hard to keep this truth in mind, especially if you're the kind of person who wants to have total control over your life. It's a little like dancing, coordinating the rhythm of your own wishes and hopes with the rhythm of the life that God may have in mind for you.

- Refresh and renew your important decisions periodically. For example, it's extremely helpful to thoughtfully and deliberately recommit yourself to your spouse every year. If you're happy in your work, do the same for that as well, and anything else in your life, from being a parent to emulating angels.

- It may seem a bit redundant at this point to advise you to make a habit of choosing good over evil. After all, you've already chosen to learn about angels and do your best to embrace some of their strengths and virtues. But, nevertheless, it's something to keep in mind. The spirit is willing, but the flesh is weak, the saying goes, and evil has a way of tempting us at least-expected moments and often in disguise.

Thought and character are one, and as character can only manifest and discover itself through environment and circumstance, the outer conditions of a person's life will always be found to be harmoniously related to his inner state. . .Humanity surges with uncontrolled passion, is tumultuous with ungoverned grief, is blown about by anxiety and doubt. Only the wise man, only he whose thoughts are controlled and purified, makes the winds and the storms of the soul obey him.

As a Man Thinketh
JAMES ALLEN

VII

THE SECOND STRENGTH
The Power of Knowing

In which you can take a giant step toward increasing your knowledge of the world, yourself, and everyone else, and start on the path to wisdom

THE INFORMATION AGE

Great knowledge is a quality of angels, far greater than anything we possess. If they are around us in abundance these days, perhaps it reflects the fact that we have entered a time in history when there has been an explosion of knowledge. Many call this the Information Age. The knowledge industry, which produces and distributes ideas and information (for instance, Yahoo and Excite on the Internet) rather than goods and services (such as Burger King or General Motors) accounted for one-quarter of the U.S. gross national product in 1955; by the late 1970s it accounted for easily one-half the total national product, and it has expanded geometrically ever since. Many of the richest people in the *Forbes* annual listing of the 400 wealthiest people in the world are information and technology moguls, in contrast to the railroad, steel, and oil barons of the Industrial Age.

This information revolution affects every one of us personally. Those of us who take the time and make the effort to educate ourselves will have a much better chance of prospering. Mastering a basic degree of technologic skill is fast becoming a necessity for personal survival. And what we're discovering, from digging in prehistoric ruins to studying the surface of furthermost planets, challenges our very souls.

From time to time, the knowledge we acquire seems to shake the very foundations of what we believe, as when we first discovered that the earth circles the sun or that it is billions of years old. Efforts to find a common ground between science and religion have emerged, as seen in a conference called "Science and the Spiritual Quest," sponsored by the John Templeton Foundation in June of 1998. "Lingering in the background of some of this soul-searching is postmodern philosophy, with its message that all belief systems, scientific and religious, are just human constructions," wrote George Johnson in the *New York Times* (Week in Review section, Sunday, July 12, 1998). He goes on, "Most religious leaders reject postmodern relativism as a dangerous threat to moral certainty. . . Some of these yearnings [for tearing down the border between science and religion] surely spring from the human compulsion to build all-embracing explanations. It's hard to abandon the hope for a system that accounts for everything, from why there is something instead of nothing to how snowflakes form. . .Given the trade-offs of both approaches, it's no wonder that each side is sometimes a little envious of the other. It's all part of the curse of never really knowing anything for sure."

It's how we use the knowledge we obtain—which is forever tentative and subject to revision—that matters, as well as our ability to go on accepting things on faith because that's the way it is.

Centuries ago Francis Bacon warned us about the risks inherent in man's pursuit of knowledge: *"The desire of power in excess caused the angels to fall, the desire of knowledge in excess caused man to fall."*

Knowledge is indeed a power, which we manage and contain only if it is effectively combined with genuine humility. In our approach to knowing, we have much to learn from angels, who are, after all, vastly superior to us in what they know and in their capacity for knowing. My emphasis in this book focuses mainly on what we can learn from angels and then on applying this to our everyday behavior. But we can also learn more *about* angels by studying ourselves, inasmuch as we already resemble them in certain ways. We are part spiritual, part angel-like. We can assume that our intellectual abilities resemble theirs, although to a much lesser degree. In other words, our ability to think logically, to reason, to intuit, to understand are miniature versions of their immense power of knowing. They simply know. We have to work to know. How much we are able to know, and the limits to how much we can absorb, assimilate, recall, and use, depends upon a central nervous system and a brain that may have been created to keep information out as much as to keep it in. Furthermore, in our efforts to learn we are always having to overcome human obstacles, such as bias, closed-mindedness, perceptions that are distorted by earlier life experiences, the noise and rattle of emotions.

We must choose to learn. This mandate doesn't apply only to our jobs or to our use of modern tools, such as computers, mobile telephones, fax machines. It urgently applies to learning as much as we can about ourselves.

A Little Knowledge of Ourselves

Who are you? There's yourself as seen through your own eyes. There's yourself as seen through the eyes of others. And then there's yourself as you really are at any given point of time. "Most of us," says Sir Henry Harcourt Reilly, in T. S. Eliot's *The Cocktail Party*, "live on a little knowledge of ourselves as we were."

You are many selves. One self is a list of incidentals connected to your physical appearance, the color of your skin, how much you weigh, how tall you are, the size of your hands and feet, even something as person-specific as your fingerprints. Another self includes your IQ, how much education you have under your belt, what skills you've acquired, your marital status, your standing with the Internal Revenue Service and your bank.

Then there's your talent self. You may be especially good at expressing yourself in words. You may possess an innate sense of rhythm and a singular appreciation of music. Your mind may be attuned to what make things tick, the basic principles of engineering. What you do with these talents—the options are innumerable—is determined by the choices you make with your free will as circumstances permit.

Another self is a mixture of inner thoughts, desires, ambitions, imaginations, drives, and the memories of a hundred major and minor life events: the big snow storm that kept you home from school, the time you won the trophy for being the star quarterback on your high school varsity team, or the first time you fell in love.

All these selves are continually in flux. What is constant is the self that constitutes your central identity. Your core. Who you have always been and will always be. What you came into this world as and what you will leave it as. Your spiritual self.

It's a lot to explore and find out about. Count on it taking you a lifetime. It's taken me one, learning who and what I am, and even now it's not complete.

How do we learn about ourselves? A bit of humble introspection helps. Sit down and review your life from time to time. Consider the more significant happenings and how you handled them. Ask yourself some pertinent questions. Are you happy? What makes you happy? What makes you sad, or discontent, or angry? Do you carry grudges? How easily do you forgive? Do you show affection to the people you love? Do you know what love is? Do you think things through? Do you live up to your responsibilities in a timely and effective way? How do you perform under pressure, like last Tuesday when it looked as if you might lose your best account? Are your feelings easily hurt? Appropriately hurt? Too often hurt? How quickly do you recover from defeat? Did you remember to send a birthday card to your sister in Seattle? Do you ever remember people's birthdays? Do you pray?

Be especially on the alert for those moments when, perhaps because there's a crisis in your life, you have a singular opportunity to learn something really important about yourself. My father's death was such an event in my life. It really shook me up. I was nearly forty. I knew he hadn't been well. The very last time I saw him, I gave him a big hug, just on impulse. *Was an angel at work?* He died shortly afterward, suddenly, of a heart attack. Now I was the father. Sure, I already was a father to four great children. But this was different. Any grievances I might have had toward him—he wasn't always an easy man, although he was always a loving one—faded away. I was flooded with good memories, and especially recollections of things he had done for me. I looked inside myself, wondering how much of him I would find there. And I felt stronger and more determined in my own identity as a father than I had ever felt before.

What have your critical moments been? What have you learned from them about the kind of person you are and want to become?

There are other ways to find out about yourself. You could even use psychological tests. A few years ago one of my friends got hold of a copy of the Myers-Briggs personality assessment test. Many of you are familiar with it, I'm sure. She began giving it to her friends so they all could compare notes after taking it. Basically, the test tells you whether you are essentially introverted (meaning you are primarily influenced by perceptions arising from within your own mind and less so by people and things around you) or extroverted (meaning the opposite, that your main source of information and stimulation comes from outside, and the people around you can have a strong effect on how you think and feel). It then assesses four personality styles, thinking, feeling, sensate, and intuitive. If you're the thinking type, you will approach most situations intellectually, attempting to figure out solutions and understand what's going on. Logic and analysis are your forte.

Let's look at how getting an idea of which type of personality you have can help you deal with things more effectively, such as overcoming a problem with procrastination. To overcome this undesirable habit, the thinking type can make out a list of things to do every morning and see that they get done. Then this person can look back and analyze his behavior and figure out exactly when and how this pattern began, which may help his efforts to change it.

The feeling type person will be inclined to look at herself in terms of emotions and values, and as she relates to other people. Without a doubt, procrastinating upsets people in her life whom she cares for and whom she doesn't want to distress. So she'd better do something about it, especially since it makes her feel anxious and depressed and think less of herself.

The sensate type of person is eminently practical. Two and two are always four. For her, the bottom line on procrastination is that she will miss out on opportunities, and she may lose his job. That's the way things are.

Finally, the intuitive type arrives at information by a method that transcends logic and does not require obvious evidence to support it. If you are intuitive, you may trust your hunches. Whether they predict good things or bad things, most of the time you're right on target. For example, you read a lot of the financial data about any company you're thinking of investing in. You don't want to go against common sense. But when the time comes to buy the stocks, you're more often right than wrong in your choices. Your decision-making process is governed by a *feeling* you get that this is the way to go.

None of us is all one style or another. But certain styles predominate. For example, I took the Myers-Briggs test and found out that I was extroverted (E), intuitive (N), and feeling (F). In evaluating how I deal with my interaction with things and people around me, it turned out I was judging (J) rather than perceiving (P), meaning that I more often use my intellect to assess situations, rather than being practical and always seeing things as they are. So I turned out to be an ENFJ, which is defined as an Extroverted Feeler with auxiliary Sensing.

That's a pretty good profile for a psychiatrist, whose job it is to care for people, interact constructively with them, intuit as well as observe what is happening, and yet be practical enough to maintain an orderly approach to his work and his life. It probably wouldn't be the best profile for an orthopedic surgeon or a postal clerk, who are more engaged with things than people in the course of their daily work.

To be sure, this kind of testing provides only a thumbnail sketch of who you really are. But it gives you a framework within which to be alert to self-discoveries that can occur at the most unexpected moments. I was talking recently with a director of a federal agency who told me he was frequently upset, irritable, and tense but couldn't figure out why. He kept his feelings to himself at work, but at home he sometimes exploded irascibly at his wife and teenage son. He thought he was an introvert, but when I explained that he couldn't be because other people seemed to have such an effect on him, he was decidedly amazed. He knew that he took a down-to-earth approach to things. He certainly cared about people, and his values were splendid. However, his major blind spot was how the employees working under him and the senior staff in the agency affected him. He experienced his days as fatiguing but couldn't figure out why.

I suggested he tell me about the most disturbing event that had happened that day or the day before. Without hesitation, he told me how one of his assistants had failed to have an important report ready for him on time. I asked him if this kind of thing happened often. "Yes," he said. "In one way or another, half the people who work for me don't do a yeoman's job. They show up late for work. They drift into meetings. Even my secretary fails to remind me sometimes of important dates I'm supposed to keep."

No wonder he was repeatedly frustrated. "To complicate matters," he went on, "I don't have very much power over them. One way or another, a lot of them have their jobs because of political connections, and, as it happens, their connections are with people who are no longer in power, which doesn't mean they don't still have power. It just means that they're disinclined to do a job for a government that they don't like." He paused thoughtfully. "I've never pieced this together before. I guess I'm going to have to expect less. . .or find a more effective way to deal with their behavior. I've been letting it drift and paying a price for it. Too tolerant, maybe. Letting my reluctance to correct people get the better of me."

That's the way we find out about ourselves—one piece of insight at a time, often provoked by some event that is upsetting, *if we are open-minded and ready to learn.* You'd be surprised to realize how many people are out of touch with their personality strengths—a generous person who feels he or she doesn't give enough to others, someone who is gifted with words but does not appreciate how well he or she can write or speak in public, a person who likes to tinker with computers but doesn't appreciate that he or she has the makings of a highly effective professional engineer.

Acquiring knowledge about yourself is a lifelong pursuit. Even angels, as remarkably intelligent as they are, cannot know all there is to know. They're not God. I'm sure they're always finding out more about themselves, unhampered by ego or pride (we know what happened to prideful angels), spurred on by angel curiosity, and comprehending with genuine humility.

GETTING TO KNOW YOU

The profession I'm in requires me to get to know a lot about what makes other people tick. I often say that reading Sherlock Holmes is probably more important for a would-be therapist than reading Freud. I have to know how people think and feel; how they thought and felt in the past; the experiences they've had throughout their lives; their hopes, ambitions, dreams, victories, and defeats. It's up to me to learn about their relationships with people around them. I have to detect the premises on which they base their perceptions and how they interpret whatever comes their way. When something goes wrong, do they feel it's their fault or someone else's fault, or that they deserve to have things go wrong because they're not very good at heart, or that it's just a matter of bad luck, or that all their luck is bad?

I have to imagine their potential, not just how they may be better able to resolve problems but the talents, behaviors, and values that can serve them well in future years, and who and what they can become if they put their minds and heart to it. Only through a growing understanding of them can I ever be of any real help.

Carrying such in-depth knowledge of others over into my personal life is a somewhat different matter. I don't read minds. My experience may permit me to recognize things in people that might escape notice by others less trained, although some people seem to have a real knack for understanding others without ever having any formal education in the process. But the relationships I have with people outside of my consulting room are with ordinary folk, not with people who have come to me and opened up their minds and hearts. No matter how close the relationship is, everyone has a circle of privacy that separates him or her from everybody else. That's no less true of good friends, husbands, wives, and children. In fact, the need to keep part of yourself hidden from sight may even be stronger in your more intimate relationships, where you may have more to lose in revealing yourself, a greater possibility of being hurt. So, in my personal world I have to work even harder at understanding others.

The first step in this process is to want to understand others. It's a matter of will. You have to care enough. Selfish people, who consistently put themselves first, are usually interested in knowing more about others only in order to satisfy their own needs and to manipulate or control others. They're a little like the fallen angels, who possess angel power but use it for ill rather than good.

Another obstacle to acquiring a genuine understanding of other people is indifference—feeling it's not worth the effort; why bother? Another is the dangerous habit of making assumptions, too often negative ones, and sticking to these even when you have evidence to the contrary. "She showed her true colors four years ago, when she broke off our relationship for a couple of months and dated someone else. Sure, she came back to me, and I took her back. But even though we're going to get married, I know I can't really trust her." Or "My husband's mean-spirited. He's irritable and short-tempered. Incommunicative. He's not a nice person. I don't care how much he tries to change, I know what he *really* is."

It never ceases to surprise me how powerful such assumptions can be in either direction, good or bad, and how resistant to any and all evidence to the contrary. "He's been unfaithful to me several times, but he's promised it won't happen again, and I believe him. He's really a good-hearted person and I know he loves me, even though he never puts it into words."

If only we had the clarity of vision of angels. But we don't. When we look at other people, our view is often clouded by our own perceptions and distortions, by clinging to the memory of past events, by hope, fear, and pessimism. The major antidote to such astigmatism is to accept that it exists and work to correct for it.

Look beyond the obvious. Create a welcoming atmosphere in which others feel free to open up to you and can trust the honesty and tolerance of your responses. Listen carefully. And if you don't understand something you're hearing, ask for it to be clarified. Try to relate what you discover to your own past experiences. Pay attention.

My work not only requires me to find out about my patients. It also forces me to consider what kind of person I am. I must examine my own thoughts and feelings, my life experiences and values. This exercise in learning does not lend itself to rash conclusions or bias, or to the imposition of my world view on those who come to me for guidance. Of course, now that I am old enough and have lived long enough to have a smattering of wisdom, I can share some of that with my patients, and with my friends, but that's quite different from telling them how they should think and what they should do. Most importantly, in my work and in my personal life, honest understanding cries out against reductionism, against pat formulas that attempt to fit everybody into a theoretical mold set up by one behavioral expert or another, whether these are published in leading medical journals or in *Redbook* or *Cosmopolitan*. *You find out what someone else is like by getting to know him or her. The emphasis is on the process of discovery.*

There's an old saying that you really don't know someone until you live with them, and even that's no guarantee. I recently asked several acquaintances how many others they could name as people who really knew them. Jerome, a married man in his early forties, replied, "My nine-year-old son." He couldn't think of anyone else. How lonely he must be, I thought, but at least he has someone. I asked Barbara, a fifty-year-old married woman, the same question. "My sister," she answered, "and my twenty-year-old daughter." What's become of intimacy between husbands and wives? I thought. Still another woman, Sally, also in her fifties, said, "No one at all." I asked myself this question and came up with a bunch of grown children, several friends, and my wife (sometimes), and I felt very fortunate indeed.

Then I turned the question around. "Whom do you think you really know well?" I asked Jerome. "My nine-year-old son, and my five-year-old too, but he's too young to really know me. My wife? I've made a career out of trying to know her. She doesn't know me, but I understand her, in what you might call an intellectual way. That's the only way our relationship has survived." When I asked Barbara, she said, "My sister and my daughter, of course. My father and mother, who were difficult people. A friend of mine, but she's pretty much into herself. My husband? I've never understood him. But it's been important for me to try to understand the people in my life. And it can take a lot out of me, sometimes. I tend to react too much to what I know. Their unhappiness can really get me down. But that's the price I pay. I wouldn't want it any other way."

I asked Sally. "No one," she said. "Nobody ever really knows anybody, in my book."

It didn't seem quite fair to ask myself to list the number of people I felt I knew, since, in a way, that's what I do for a living. But what about the people in my personal life? How well do I know them? None completely. I'm always alert to finding out new things about all of them. My wife? Yes (sometimes not). Certainly my children. Half a dozen friends. And I know enough about a great many other people to decide whether I want to spend time with them, get to know them better, do business with them, trust them.

Knowing someone is the basis of trust, without which no relationship can survive and flourish. When I was driving my youngest daughter to college on her first day there, I asked her if she wanted any sage advice. She shook her head. "Well, I'm going to give you some anyway." She cringed a little. "Let me tell you something about trust. Trust isn't given. It's earned. You're going to meet a lot of young people at school. Many of them are going to dress like you and talk like you and even share a lot of your interests, and you'll be tempted to trust them pretty quickly, because trusting people is something all of us want to do, except for chronically distrustful people, and we don't fit that category. DON'T!" She looked surprised. "What I mean is that trust is earned. It doesn't just happen. Even though the people you're going to meet look pretty good on the surface, their values and motivations may be quite different from yours, and yours are really good. Their perception of reality may be light-years away from your own. It takes time. You have to get to know them before you can put any serious trust in them. And you'll find that some are trustworthy, but others aren't. Knowing them is what makes all the difference."

"That's pretty good advice, Dad," she replied.

Knowing someone is at the very heart of loving. Beyond infatuation (which contains great elements of illusion), beyond passion (originating in very basic hormonally governed instincts, and also enhanced by imagination), beyond similarities (we both like the Beatles and going to the beach in the summertime), beyond proximity (otherwise known as the girl next door or sitting at the next computer station), it is knowing one another that establishes the intimacy needed for love to be born, grow, and endure.

A long-standing friend of mine recently asked if I would talk with his daughter Rebecca and her husband, in their late thirties, who were having problems in their marriage. She was considering divorce, something my friend thought was a rash move and completely unwarranted. Would I be willing to spend an hour with them, maybe offer them some suggestions, see whether marriage counseling (with someone else, since I was such a good friend of Rebecca's parents) would be worth undertaking?

After some initial conversation, during which time I learned a little about each of them I hadn't known before, Rebecca informed me that she had been unhappy for several years, and she had thought of divorce, but it wasn't what she really wanted. "What happened to the feelings we used to have toward each other?" her husband, Rick, asked. "They're gone," she said sadly. "How can I feel any love or affection toward you when I've been hurt so often by your temper outbursts. . .and your complete inability to understand my feelings?"

"I know you very well, Becky," Rick said with a tone of annoyance. "As well as I can know someone who never talks about her feelings." "You never ask about them," she said curtly.

"Tell me, Becky," I asked, "when Rick lost his cool and blew up about something or other, did you let him know how hurtful this was to you? Or did you keep it to yourself?" Rebecca nodded, looking slightly embarrassed. "I expected him to realize that for himself. Is that too much to hope for?"   "Probably, most of the time, with most people," I replied.

"Rick," I said, looking at him, "if you suspected that something was bothering Rebecca, why wouldn't you ever ask her about it?" He responded abruptly. "I didn't have to ask her. It was obvious. *I* bothered her." I raised my hands and made a calming gesture in his direction. "It would have been a lot better to ask her and wait for her answer. So what is she telling you now? That your outbursts, like this one a few seconds ago, upset her. Hardly a mystery."

I turned to Rebecca. "On the other hand, you say you never let him know what you felt in ways he could understand. You can't be expected to be understood if you don't communicate. And you, Rick, you can't expect to understand if you don't inquire and listen to what you're hearing." In the silence that followed, I could see them giving thought to what had just happened.

"I'm sorry," he whispered.

"I am too," she said, reaching out to take his hand.

"Okay. This is a good beginning. You've both learned something important about each other, here, in just under an hour. If it sticks, fine. If not, maybe you should have some counseling. Give me a ring in a few weeks and let me know how things are going, and, if you want, I'll give you the name of someone you can see." Would that most people I deal with demonstrated as much flexibility and good will as Rebecca and Rick.

Knowing is the basis of loving, and love is what makes us want to know more and more about those we love.

ORIGINAL THINKING

The Greeks once believed that creative ideas were instilled in artists and great thinkers by the muses. We have always considered some of our greatest writers and poets as being inspired in a special way, although nowadays we tend to assume that such genius comes from within the creative individual rather than from some invisible external force. We are willing to admit that one person can inspire another, or even that circumstances can stimulate original thought and action. But, in general, we no longer look to spirits as influencing the special insights and perspectives that brilliant minds seem to produce. The world has grown disturbingly focused on mankind as the center of the universe, which may be one reason why we have been given a glimpse of earth from outer space, a small planet circling in its orbit, and the possibility of other solar systems where intelligent life may exist. To believe in human beings as all there is seems foolish. It may be that there are muses out there after all, called angels.

Angels possess powerful intellect. They must be creative, since creativity is one of the highest functions of thought.

Now, only God can create something from nothing. Even angels can't do that. But that's not the kind of creativity I'm talking about. Creativity is essentially the ability to combine old ideas in new ways, to see reality from a totally different perspective. All learning involves creativity. Children who discover for the first time that they are separate from their mothers, individuals in their own right, who learn to walk and talk and tie shoes and find their way home when seemingly lost, are engaged in creative behavior no less than the first impressionist painter who deserted the strict confines of reality to share his own mental image of what he was seeing. As we grow older, however, a lot of unlearning has to precede relearning, and this calls for a good deal of flexibility in one's mental machinery.

To become more angel-like, we should begin to value creativity in our own lives. We must think of ourselves as being, to some degree, blessed with creative potential. This does not mean that most of us are going to invent a new theory of physics, like Einstein, or win a Nobel prize for literature. What it does mean is that we can make creative thinking a habit in our approach to everyday life. If you are faced with a serious problem that seems overwhelming and to which there seems to be no obvious solution, you can give up, stew in a hopeless state of worry and futility, or bring your creative energies to bear on the situation until you find the light.

I have written extensively on the subject of creativity in many other places. I won't repeat myself here. But I will offer a few suggestions that you may follow to start introducing angel-like creativity into your thinking. Begin by appreciating the fact that you are creative, whether you've developed this strength yet or not. Open the doors of your mind; be receptive to new ideas. This does not mean filling your mind with all the trash modern communication vehicles offer you. Be highly selective in what you watch on television or in film and in what you read. Carefully choose the company you keep, because other people can dishearten you in your efforts to think creatively, or they can berate you, put your ideas down, destroy your efforts with rapid-fire criticism and ridicule. In other words, surround yourself with people who behave like angels and offer others inspiration, patience, and encouragement.

It doesn't matter whether you're trying to find yourself in your career, or to figure out how to improve a love relationship or communicate with your children, or to fix up your house so it really reflects you, or to locate the right doctor, or to manage your money, or to set up a plan for your retirement. You can meet all these challenges and more, if you make creativity a strong and easily accessible habit of mind.

Years ago I was stranded in the O'Hare airport in Chicago in the middle of a blizzard. All flights were being canceled, including mine to New York. One plane was still going to take off. It was headed for Phoenix. Now, the ordinary way to think would be to say to yourself, I'm traveling east, not west, so why should I even pay attention to a flight heading to Arizona. A light went on in my head. Get that flight and go to Phoenix, and you'll be in New York before any plane takes off again here. I had to satisfy myself with having come up with an unusual solution to my dilemma, because by the time I had reached the ticket counter, the gates were closed and the plane was already taxiing for take off. But, stimulated by my first idea, I had another. I could imagine the pandemonium that would run rampant in the airport as it filled the next morning with endless lines of men and women trying to get outbound flights as soon as the snow had been cleared. I headed for a telephone and called my travel agent at home. He arranged a reservation for me for the next day, so I would be spared the confusion and inevitable delays to which I would otherwise have been subjected.

There are a few ground rules to follow to develop a habit of creative behavior. For example, if you're searching for a new idea, don't automatically accept the first idea you come up with. Reach for more, sometimes many more. Because the more ideas you allow to enter your mind, the more likely you'll be to come up with ones that are different and that will really work to solve the problem you are facing.

And don't evaluate and judge your ideas one at a time. Let them flow, until you have a bunch of them. Only then take a hard look and decide which ones make any sense and appear to be promising. And if you need more ideas, simmer for a while. Put the problem aside and let your subconscious do some work on its own. Then, armed with more ideas, choose one or more of the better ones and try them out, testing them against reality to see if they do the job.

If you're an introvert, you'll probably do your most creative thinking alone. Incidentally, you are much more likely to come up with ideas that are genuinely original since you won't be so influenced by what others think or by the way things are supposed to be. If, on the other hand, you're an extrovert, you may find you do your best creative thinking interacting with others. Their input stimulates you, even though some of your most valuable ideas may occur to you later, when you are by yourself. Or ideas may pop into your head at the most unexpected times, such as when you're driving on the freeway, or waking up from a dream in the middle of the night, or having dinner with a couple of friends, or lying on a beach warming yourself in the sun and listening to the roll of the breakers.

Call these sudden flashes inspiration, and thank your angel for them, because that may be where your best new ideas have come from.

GUIDELINES FOR MODELING OURSELVES AFTER ANGELS

Knowing

- Commit yourself (*an act of free will*) to a lifetime of learning. Continue to educate yourself, not only in the technical, business, or professional requirements of your work, but with regard to the broad canvas of human experience. Improve your vocabulary. Read good literature. Listen to good music. Think about life's meaning. Master a sport, if you're so inclined.

Find a hobby or avocation in which you can discover refreshment for body, mind, and soul.

- Keep in mind that knowing is more than possessing information. It is open-mindedness and receptivity to discovery, holding on to the capacity for the surprise and delight of childhood, no matter how old you are.

- Practice your learning power. Inquire. Listen. Observe. Delve into things. Be alert to new insights and ideas, especially to inspiration.

- Make learning about yourself and others a number-one priority, and don't be blinded by false assumptions in the process.

- See ignorance for the evil it is. In Charles Dicken's classic tale *A Christmas Carol*, there is a scene in which the regally attired Ghost of Christmas Present—most likely an angel—spreads his heavy robes, revealing two children huddling at his feet, a boy and a girl. "This boy is ignorance," he says. "This girl is want. Beware these children, Ebenezer Scrooge. But most of all, beware this boy!"

- Use your knowledge, your power to know, and your creativity only for good ends. Think kindly, hopefully, unselfishly, courageously, lovingly. Stay far away from destructive thoughts that generate dishonesty, confusion, accusation, betrayal, violence, and self-indulgence, lest, regardless of how materially successful you are, happiness and spirituality elude you.

Let me not to the marriage of true minds
Admit impediments; love is not love
Which alters when it alteration finds,
Or bends with the remover to remove
O, no, it is an ever-fixed mark
That looks on tempests, and is never shaken;
It is the star to every wand'ring bark,
Whose worth's unknown, although his height be
taken.
Love's not Time's fool, though rosy lips and cheeks
Within his bending sickle's compass come;
Love alters not with his brief hours and weeks,
But bears it out even to the edge of doom.
   If this be error and upon me proved,
   I never writ, nor no man ever loved.

Sonnet 116
WILLIAM SHAKESPEARE

VIII

THE THIRD STRENGTH
Love and Generosity

In which you will achieve a new understanding of love and of the joy of being a real live altruist

PROBABLY NO subject has received as much attention as love. This could be because, sometimes, there seems to be so little of it around in the world. But I prefer to think that it is because people really realize how central love is to our very existence. Jesus Christ's message was one of love. St. Paul spoke of faith, hope, and love and emphasized that love was the greatest of these virtues. Love fills our poetry—sweet love, lost love, unrequited love, sacred love. It seems that love is what every human being needs in order to grow up whole, as if through the experience of having been on the receiving end of love, one learns to give love to others.

There are a couple of things about love you would do well to keep in mind. First, you can approximate its depth from your own feelings and behavior and from those of another person, but you can't literally measure it. You can't say, I have fourteen pounds of love toward you, but you only have eight pounds toward me. It doesn't work that way. It's true that between two people at one time or another, one loves more and the other not as much. This can be explained by a wide variety of reasons, many of which have nothing to do with love itself, such as unresolved hurts, or worries, or just plain fatigue—several more human frailties for which allowances must be made.

The second point is that love grows when it is returned and dies when there is no reciprocity. Anyone who thinks he or she can go on loving someone who does not love him or her is either mad or a fool, although you can love the memory of what you may have once had with each other. Love that works and grows over time requires that the energy and caring be a two-way street.

LOVE IS CARING

The strict definition of love is simply caring. You and I each have our own definition of what love is. Some of us reserve the word to describe that special feeling, akin to infatuation, that makes another person seem unique and worth being cherished, a feeling filled with excitement and pleasure that reaches down into the core of our being. We want to be near that person. We are entranced by how he or she appears, the sound of his or her voice, the sparkle in the eyes, the smile. It's magical. It can even be painful when we are apart, or when our love is not returned.

A FAMILY AFFAIR

Love is also a family affair—between husbands and wives, among parents and children. It's less special but certainly less intense. In fact, nobody could attend to the everyday responsibilities of life in a perpetual state of enchantment. You'd forget your appointments, burn dinner on the stove, maybe even get hit by a bus crossing the street. Unfortunately, family love is often taken too much for granted. Birthdays and holidays bring attention to it, with phone calls and greeting cards and presents. But its real presence is to be found in the give and take of life, in listening to each other, in offering advice and reassurance, in helping children with their homework, in paying the bills, in looking after the material, emotional, and spiritual needs of all concerned. Just being there for each other, cheering each other on, even offering each other a critique or two to help each be a better person.

LOVING FRIENDS

Then there are friends, people we enjoy spending time with, with whom we have a lot in common. These are the people we share our innermost feelings with, on whom we can depend, and who can depend on us. Loyalty. We give each other the support to endure the storms of life over time. Few things please me more than to know that one of my own closest friends dates back to when I was twenty years old, and that the ups and downs of life have only made our relationship richer for wear. (I used to have friends who dated back further than that, but when you reach a certain age, that privilege becomes a bit harder to maintain.)

LOVE THE WORLD AROUND US

We love things, too. Patriotism is love of country. You can love a good meal or a good book, or a fine film, especially one about angels. I recently visited Muir Woods, north of San Francisco, for the first time. I spent an hour in the presence of the colossal redwood trees, seemingly reaching up forever toward the sky, their trunks so massive you could stretch out your arms and still not match their width. More than once I placed the palm of my hand on the bark of a tree and felt a sense of communion with this magnificent living creature, perhaps a thousand years old.

That Muir Woods even exists for me to visit is the result of an act of unusual generosity. I'd call it an example of true altruism.

In the early part of the twentieth century, William Kent made a gift of Redwood Canyon, north of San Francisco, to the federal government. Theodore Roosevelt, who was president at the time, wrote to Kent, thanking him for the "groves of giant trees," adding, "my dear sir, this is your gift. . .I should greatly like to name the monument the Kent Monument, if you will permit it."

Kent replied, "I thank you from the bottom of my heart for your message. . .and hope and believe it will strengthen me to go on in an attempt to save more of the precious and vanishing glories of nature for a people too slow of perception. Your kind suggestion of a change of name is not one that I can accept. So many millions of better people have died forgotten, that to stencil one's own name on a benefaction seems to carry with it an implication of mundane immortality, as being something purchasable. . .I have this day sent you by mail a few photographs of [what I wish to be called] Muir Woods."

John Muir was a pioneer environmentalist, devoted to the preservation of the redwoods and all things in nature, and someone that William Kent felt was more deserving of being remembered than himself. Kent may have known that memorials, as fine as they may be, have little significance in the realm where angels dwell, toward which our journey takes us all.

I WISH YOU WELL!

Of course, since angels are pure will, intellect, and spirit, we can be angel-like in our love only to the extent that it involves these three elements. Peter Kreeft, author of *Angels (and Demons)* points out that charity, or willing the good of the other, comes from the will rather than from feelings, and that, since angels have will, it's this kind of love that they manifest. "They are altruists," he writes. "They will the good of other angels. . .and the good of the humans whom they guard as 'guardian angels.'"

What a powerful concept this is for us all: to will the good of others! Take a minute to think of all the people in your life, and whisper (or shout, if you want), "I wish you all well!" Doesn't that feel good? Doesn't that dispel some of the hurt and resentment over past slights and misunderstandings that have been corroding your soul and perhaps helping to clog up your arteries with heavy cholesterol? It goes a long way toward counteracting the effects of hate, envy, and, especially in this nation today, competition raging out of control. "I wish you well."

Angels are also intellect. That is to say, they know, and knowledge plays a vital role in the experience of loving. It once puzzled me that in Hebrew Scriptures, "to know" someone meant to be emotionally and physically intimate with that person. But the more I considered it, the more relevant the term became. True love is far from blind. Intimacy is an inherent part of love. To be intimate, you must truly know the person you love. Because we are human beings and not angels, such knowing can never be perfect. It is an ongoing process of knowing more and more about that person, and maybe what we learn isn't always that great. But, on balance, good outweighs the not-so-good, and love goes on.

KNOWING THE ONE YOU LOVE

Knowing and the intimacy that knowing provides are what distinguish true love from mere passion. Sexual ecstasy can hardly endure in the absence of knowing. Sexual passion is part and parcel of the love relationship between two people who have committed themselves to each other, to be faithful in their devotion, but it is only the special quality of love, a spiritual quality, that can keep passion alive and well amid the stress and strain of human living.

Knowing is also the basis of empathy, whereby we understand what the person we love is experiencing and are able to comfort or encourage him or her, leading to a deepening of love. It is the basis of trust, without which love cannot survive. It provides us with common sense, so that we do not persist in an insane commitment to someone who does not love us, who may be inherently selfish, or who might just succeed in driving us out of our minds. (It's no surprise that a great many divorces take place among men and women who marry at a very young age without sufficient knowledge of the persons they are marrying.) And knowing is the enemy of codependency, a contemporary term used to describe the relationship between someone who is addicted to drugs, alcohol, or other destructive behavior patterns, and an enabler who is locked into a relationship that serves only to keep the problems alive, and more often to make things much worse.

THE SPIRIT OF LOVE

Finally, of course, angels are spiritual. Spirituality is the better part of ourselves, and the better part of love. However, it is this aspect of love that we humans often find the hardest to incorporate in our experience of loving. Physical love? That's easy to define. Psychological love? That comes with the territory. But spiritual love? First you have to acknowledge your own spirituality. Then you have to appreciate the spiritual reality of someone else, the person you love. And you have to make a connection. Transcendence? One meaning of transcendence is "to exist apart from the material universe." That's angel-like love, knowing within your own spirit that the people you love are spirit too, setting the stage for a respect, a reverence, an awe, an excitement all its own.

As you strive to become more angel-like in your loving, keep in mind that we are not angels. As human beings, it's our job to integrate the intellectual and spiritual qualities of love within the context of our humanity. I recently saw a couple in their fifties who had been married for nearly thirty years. Sex and romance had fled their marriage. Even casual expressions of affection had long since disappeared. They were both unhappy with the way they were. They *knew* something had to be done. They were *willing* to give it a try. It took only half a dozen meetings to produce what looked like a miracle. It's quite rare that we doctors get such quick and meaningful results. Our conversations centered on helping them see how the ordinary strains of life had conspired to make them too tired to feel love. They'd been busy for years, working, raising a family. Now their children were grown and gone. They were alone. And they were worn out. I can't say what really happened, only that in the course of nine hours together, somehow we rekindled a spark that led to renewed affection, friendship, and sexual passion as well. I did ask them to tell me what had attracted each to the other in the first place, thereby reawakening happy memories of being young and very much in love. They had understandably changed in their appearance, but when I asked what each saw when they looked at the other, their answers did not seem to be that much different from how saw each other the first time they met.

I am reminded of an old movie, *The Enchanted Cottage*, with Robert Young and Dorothy McGuire. Robert Young plays a soldier who has returned home having been blinded in the war. Dorothy McGuire plays the role of a plain woman, destined to be an "old maid." They fall in love and marry. And they live in a magic cottage where only they perceive each other as beautiful. That's what happens when people are really in love and possess spiritual love. When Shakespeare so aptly wrote about loving outlasting the ravages of time, it was spiritual love he must have had in mind.

More on the spirituality of love

Spiritual love plays no less a role in the relationship that exists between friends. Many friendships are limited in time and place. You may room with a friend in college, or share a foxhole with one on the front lines. You may work with a friend, day in and day out, on the job. You may live next door to a friend and play tennis together at the local health club every Saturday. But when you graduate, or when the war is over, or when you change jobs or move to a new neighborhood, most of these friendships fade away.

But not all. Some friendships seem to last forever. When they do, they represent more than mutual regard, companionship, or camaraderie. A spiritual element is added to these. It doesn't seem to matter how many years have passed or how much regular contact there is, these relationships go on. Stop for a moment and count how many such friendships you may have in your life.

I've done that and come up with four. I met one friend in college; he was my best man at my wedding. Another went to medical school with me. Another, a minister, entered my life when I was forty, at a time when I was particularly stressed and distressed, when my life had seemed to fall apart; he helped me build a new one, through his empathy and spirituality. Now that I think about it, he may have been sent by an angel. In 1974 a fourth close friend heard the first chapter of my just-published book, *The Secret Strength of Depression*, on his car radio as he was driving from Connecticut to New York City. He called and asked to meet me. We've been friends ever since. In every one of these friendships, something beyond personal similarities, having common interests, and sharing important life experiences and values, has made them both rich and enduring. And you don't have to look very far to realize it's something spiritual.

In fact, spirituality enters into every human relationship, even those involving passing acquaintances, shopkeepers, bank tellers, restaurant waiters, strangers on the street, and strangers in far-off lands. When Jesus said that we should love our neighbor as ourselves and was asked, "Who is my neighbor?" he told the familiar parable of the Good Samaritan, who stopped to aid an injured Israelite. The crucial point of the parable is that the Samaritans and Jews were enemies, but that didn't stop the Samaritan from lending a helping hand. In other words, everyone is our neighbor and deserving of our spiritual love, regardless of race, color, creed, and nationality. There are no bigots among the angels.

This doesn't mean you have to like everyone or want to spend any time with them. They may even live in another part of the world, and except for television and pictures in magazines you may never see them in person. They may even be your enemy, and you may have to take whatever steps are necessary to protect yourself from them.

Still you can—and must—love them spiritually. This involves respect for them as spiritual fellow beings, and all that such respect implies. They all have guardian angels whispering in their ears, telling them to have the same kind of love for you. Whether they choose to hear is another matter. But you can listen, and love.

GUIDELINES FOR MODELING OURSELVES AFTER ANGELS

Love and Generosity

- Make the phrase "I wish you well" a continuous theme in your mind and heart. Think and feel toward others: I want you to be happy; I want you to be well; I want you to prosper; I want you to be loved; I want you to recognize your talents and fulfill them.

  Within this context, it will become so much easier to communicate at all levels with those you love, to offer encouragement, even to offer constructive and far more acceptable critiques when these are warranted. After all, who can fail to appreciate hearing the sincere well-wishes of someone who isn't just saying things out of pure self-interest? "I wish you well" can go a long way toward reducing the all-too-common fault of putting others down, of focusing on what's wrong and seldom acknowledging what's good about them.

- Practice generosity until it becomes second nature to you. Be more giving of your time, energy, thought, and possessions. I recall a fund-raiser once advocating that we should give "until it hurts." That's silly advice. The habit of giving is one of life's great pleasures. Of course, don't be foolish about it, trying to be so altruistic that you seriously neglect your own needs or run up huge deficits on your credit cards, or thinking that charity primarily consists of giving money to nonprofit organizations. Charity does begin at home, right at your own doorstep. It's a virtue to be measured by its sincerity, not its size. I knew a wealthy family whose members, when it came to donating wings of hospitals or great sums to universities, seemed to know no limits, as long as their names were inscribed in big, bold letters over every building they endowed. But they treated each other miserably. When it came to simply wishing each other well, they failed completely.

- Whenever you pass a homeless person who asks you for money, don't pass him or her by or think unkind thoughts. Drop a quarter in the cup.

- Say hello to a tree.

- Think all year long about birthday and holiday and special occasion presents for those you love, and buy them when it occurs to you. You can find a place to hide them until the day arrives.

• Recognize and rid yourself of any selfish tendencies. Selfishness is the complete antithesis of altruism. It's not listed as one of the seven deadly sins, but it probably should be. Maybe it's pride's cousin. Me first, last, and always. Selfish people rarely admit to their selfishness. That's one of the things that makes living with them so very disheartening—and disabling. The people who are part of a selfish individual's life end up like wounded soldiers in a field hospital, bruised and bandaged in their souls, and often their bodies too, since selfishness is a main contributor to physical as well as mental abuse. If you are selfish, ultimately you will find yourself alone, although you may be so absorbed in yourself that you won't care very much, except for not having anyone to take care of you when you're old. Nor will you be able to join the angels, and you will leave in your wake one very disappointed and defeated angel who had been assigned as your guardian in this life (another victim of your self-love, who may not earn his wings this time around).

• Watch the film of A Christmas Carol, the old black-and-white version starring Alistair Sims as Scrooge. I've seen it a dozen times and never fail to be excited and moved by its power. Scrooge is the prototype of the stingy, ungiving man. As you probably know, he is visited by three ghosts (angels) on Christmas Eve. The ghost of Christmas past reminds him of his life as it had been, of the young man of promise who had vanished in a sea of resentment and greed. The ghost of Christmas present shows him the joy that others have in their love for one another. The ghost of Christmas yet to come gives him a glimpse of his own ignominious end, pointing at his tombstone as Scrooge cries and pleads and begs for this not to be his fate. He awakens to find himself in his own bed and realizes that the spirits have done their work in a single night. It is Christmas morning. He can act at once on the illuminations he has been given (angels are messengers, are they not? and we frequently receive their messages as sudden insights or dreams). Scrooge jumps around with joy, opens his window and leans out and shouts to a boy standing below in the snow-covered street to rush to the grocer and buy a goose that hangs there and deliver it to Tiny Tim's family. He has taken his first step toward becoming angel-like, a new, loving, and charitable human being.

• When you love somebody, let him or her know, maybe by a gentle touch now and then, spontaneous and unstudied. How often do you say, "I love you"? The words can sometimes come hard, even though your feelings of love may run deep. Maybe you're constrained by shyness, or are embarrassed to express such sentiments. Don't be. Put words to your love— romantic love; love between lovers; between husbands and wives; between sons, daughters, and parents; between brothers and sisters; between friends. Of course, each relationship represents a different kind of love and calls for its own form of expression. And you don't have to be boring about it. Use your imagination to find other phrases that mean the same thing, such as "You're special" or "I adore you" or "You mean so much to me" or "I couldn't ask for a finer son" or "I'm so happy to have you as a daughter." There are an infinite number of ways to let someone else know how much you care. Actions speak louder than words, and your day-to-day behavior addresses the point. But all of us like to hear an old-fashioned "I love you" from someone who genuinely means it and whom we love in return.

If poets [we] are not listened to, the
        blame
is theirs. They speak unclearly,
        and are lost
In their own psychic maze and
        the intricate game
        Of words. In a twisted world
                what matters most
Is simple statement, open to the
                least
                Of men. . .
                        . . .The obscure
Is powerless over violence. Each
        word
        Must be inevitable, urgent, pure
        If people are to hear, above the
                roar
The voice of those who know
        what speech is for.

From *Eighteen Poems*

JAMES BOYD

IX

THE FOURTH STRENGTH

Communicating

*In which you will begin to master the art of local
(person-to-person) and long distance (here-to-heaven) transmission*

ANGELS ALWAYS seem to be busy delivering messages. It's their most apparent habit, telling us things that God wishes us to know. One thing is for sure. When they are about their business, they are brief, succinct, clear, and purposeful, nothing like the endless parade of talking heads on television you'll come across when you're channel surfing. It's ironic that at this stage in our evolution, with such marvelous tools with which to communicate, we seem to have less and less to say that has much meaning. Even good entertainment is hard to come by.

Yet communication is the very essence of living. In the early morning in the country you can hear the plaintive "hoo hoo" of the mourning dove, and in the late afternoon dozens of sparrows fill the trees and the sky with their chirping. A stranger (not an angel) sneaks around the back of your house, and your Irish setter starts to bark loudly, an angry bark, not the greeting you get from him when you come home after work. Sometimes, when I hear the wind blowing through the leaves of tall locust trees, I can't help but wonder if they too are saying something to each other, beyond my comprehension.

DNA communicates too. It tells the cells in our bodies what to do. It determines how tall we will be, the color of our eyes, the precise characteristics of our fingerprints, how well our kidneys and brains will function and for how long, how healthy we may be, when we will grow old, and even when we may die.

Up the evolutionary scale, from whispering locust trees to human beings, minds, body, and spirit, communication is connectedness. It has the same origin as words (and concepts) such as *communion and community*. It implies a togetherness. It's what enables us to learn and grow and survive. I don't have to spell out for you the many ways in which communication plays a vital role in our lives from infancy to old age. Nor do I have to tell you that our communication skills represent a combination of an innate, genetically determined capacity; what happens to us, and how we react to and act to influence our environment; and the efforts we put into learning how to do communicate.

Language is a remarkable gift, one that we should cherish and not allow to fall into disuse. How we speak reveals a good deal about who we are. If English is our language, for instance, our manner of speech may be a clue as to where we hail from—South Carolina, Brooklyn, the Scottish Highlands, or Australia. Some of us are garrulous, going on at length about nothing in particular. Or we may be people of few words. We may be primarily concerned with what *we* are saying. Or we may pay appropriate attention to someone who is talking to us. We may even talk to ourselves, sometimes out loud.

There's no point in enumerating all the things we talk about. You're quite familiar with them. Human relationship is a very popular topic. So are health and money and current events, movies and books and sports, and work. Sometimes we just want to make contact. I was sitting in a coffee shop on Father's Day, for example, and there must have been half a dozen people on their cellular phones calling home to let their fathers know they were thinking about them and wishing them well.

We put our emotions into words. It's a lot better to scream and yell when you're mad about something than to punch the wall and hurt your fist, or strike out at someone else. I often consider that the strength of the United Nations is its assembly of delegates from every nation in the world, who can express their grievances in words, thus hopefully reducing the likelihood of doing so by going to war. You can verbally express anger, grief, joy, sadness, even fear. You can solicit empathy by putting your unhappiness into words. You can find support when you share your fears with someone else.

How shall we use this marvelous gift to communicate? To spread joy, of course. To accentuate the positive. To praise and express our love and encourage others in their efforts to do good. The last thing we should do is radiate a negative energy that depletes others of their joy, self-confidence, self-esteem—for their sakes, and for our own, because that's a sure way to end up unhappy, pessimistic, lonely. My advice is to bite your tongue and deftly excise sarcasm, caustic remarks, and fault-finding from your repertoire. Everyone will be happier, especially yourself.

DON'T CRITICIZE; CRITIQUE INSTEAD

There is a proper place and time to use your communication skills to offer criticism. Unfortunately, the word *criticism* itself can mean to "carp" or "reproach." I like the word critique much better, because it suggests that you have noticed or even studied something or someone, and then decided to make your observations known. A book or film review is a critique. A teacher critiques his or her students. Parents often criticize their children when they would do well to critique them instead. Later on in life, grown children may even critique their parents.

The distinction I make between criticizing and critiquing is that the former has an inherently destructive power, whereas the latter is designed to express love and caring, and is truly made for the benefit of the person being critiqued. None of us is perfect—far from it. In fact, we can be very imperfect at times. From table manners to misjudgments, we operate within the confines of our human nature. Ignorance is one such limitation. Not caring enough is another. Lacking insight into ourselves is yet another. So how can we learn if things aren't pointed out to us? Critiquing is a necessary process.

To critique successfully, you need to acquire the skill to communicate clearly and to encourage the other person to welcome the advice and not feel put down. You also have to have the authority to critique. Is it your place to do so? Do you have the knowledge? Do you have the skills? Can you do so out of love, concern, or friendship for the other person? Can you stick to the matter at hand? Has the other consented to your role? In medicine, we are now required to obtain an informed consent from all patients on whom we intend to do any diagnostic or treatment procedure. That would be a bit much in ordinary human affairs, but it has its place. Is the other person really open to hearing what you have to say and learning from it? Is it the right time? Should you initiate a discussion or wait until your opinion is requested? (Sound familiar?) Who should tell Martha about the way she dresses? Are you the one to deal with Harry's not doing his homework on time?

When should "who" tell George he should really do something about his weight? Jim, why don't you see that Alice isn't going to make a commitment to you; you really should break it off. Bill, I'd like to talk with you about your constant use of four-letter words instead of speaking plain English. Sally, you're not doing the kind of work I expect of you. What's wrong? Can I do anything to help?

We can all use more knowledge about ourselves. We'd do well to welcome valuable insights, and to prevent personal sensitivities from keeping us from hearing what is being told to us in an honest way and for our own good.

Truth, or consequences of the lie

We can speak the truth, or we can lie. Most of us will occasionally exaggerate the details of a story to make it more interesting. A novel isn't true, but it's not a lie. Everybody knows it's fiction. It says so right on the jacket. Lying is something else. Lying defeats the whole purpose of communication itself.

Can you imagine an angel telling a lie? In Genesis, for example, can you imagine the angel telling Abraham that his wife, Sarah, would bear him a son, only to have Abraham discover that this was not true? Or what if Raphael told Tobias that the road ahead was safe and suggested Tobias go first, so that he might fall into a deep hole and be trapped there? Or can you picture the angel of the Lord reassuring Paul that he and the crew of his ship would weather the storm, when the angel knew all along that every man aboard was going to drown?

We can understand the lie only if we understand the nature of truth, which defeats the whole purpose of communication itself. Synonyms for the word *truth* are revealing: genuineness, integrity, reality, fact. *Truth means saying it as it is, or at least not saying it as it isn't.* Some truths are obvious. Human beings are supposed to have two arms, two legs, two eyes, two ears, one stomach, and one heart, and most of the time they do. If you heat water to 212 degrees Fahrenheit, it will boil. The shortest distance between two points is a straight line. The world is shaped like an egg, even though until relatively recently most people thought it to be flat, showing that what is not true may be perceived as true until it is shown to be otherwise.

Unless we are scientists engaged in complex research, we seldom face dilemmas of truth that involve the evaluation of obvious fact. The truths that affect us are of a more personal nature. "Where were you on

Thursday evening?" Here's a question that might be put to you by a district attorney attempting to prove you guilty of some crime (remember, you're under oath, and in this setting a lie constitutes perjury), or by an angry spouse who suspects you of infidelity. Or it might be a casual question asked by a friend who was trying to reach you on the telephone all evening. "How much did you pay for that dress?" "How old are you, really?" "What do you think of Diane's new boyfriend?" "Why did you take so much money out of the joint account?" Or it may surround a work-related matter. "This is a great report. . .did you really prepare this all by yourself?" "Whose idea was it to go ahead with that new product that's done so well in the marketplace?" It may be something very basic to your life: "Do you love me?"

Truth obviously does not always involve a response to an inquiry. You can volunteer the truth in telling what you've been up to or you can withhold it, which, if the person you're talking to has a right to know the truth, is itself a form of lying. I have a friend who said he used to shade the truth. He was in his second marriage. Although his new wife seemed genuinely fond of his eleven-year-old son by his former wife, she could, at times, get very angry at him, accusing him of spending too much time with the boy and not enough with her. So to avoid risking a scene, he got into the habit of telling his wife he had some errands to run, when, on an occasional Saturday afternoon, he actually would take his son out to lunch and a movie. "I do have an important errand to run," he thought, justifying to himself what he told her, "being with my son." Nonetheless he felt strained and uncomfortable in his concealment, and his uneasiness communicated itself to his wife. It didn't take her long to guess what was going on. A horrible scene ensued, the two of them shouting back and forth for an hour without any resolution. When he discussed his problem with me, I told him straight out that he would have been better off telling her that he intended to see the boy every couple of weeks at the very least and asking her to accept that gracefully. The thought of doing this made him very nervous.

"What if she gets angry at me?" he asked.

"Then she gets angry at you," I said. "But it won't be for fudging the truth. Besides, what kind of relationship can you two have if you're afraid to tell her anything that might upset her?"

Hesitantly he took my advice and tried to be upfront whenever he planned to see his son. She wasn't happy about it at first. She felt as if time spent with the boy was time taken away from her. She also worried that he might still have feelings for his former wife. She was quick to criticize. When she did, she often became sarcastic, which was one reason he had found it difficult to be open and honest with her. Now he began to stand his ground without losing his temper. As he did so, she seemed unexpectedly reassured, and she gradually became less and less disturbed about the time he spent with his son.

Of course, you can be telling an untruth without being fully aware of it, because what you are saying is something you incorrectly believe to be correct. *Emotions readily interfere with our perceptions of reality.* This isn't always bad. After all, enthusiasm often involves an element of distortion. When you think a particular man is a prince charming or a woman has the grace of an angel, these impressions are usually not strictly the way things are. Deep down you know this, but your feelings overpower your logic. Besides, you may delight in your misperception. That's fine, as long as you know what's going on.

I have also seen plenty of situations in which emotions get the better of truth, and destructively so. For example, I've known a number of people who seriously malign their ex-spouses, grossly exaggerating faults and failings, reflecting genuine hurt and anger they have not yet been able to free themselves of; or, sometimes mobilizing an intense hostility, they seem to need to go ahead with a divorce in order to justify their actions. I have known people who have been victimized by dishonest investment advisors motivated by greed (not an emotion in the strict sense of the word, but certainly a compelling force for lying). I have know women who have been seduced by false promises of love by men whose only motive was their own sexual pleasure.

Distorting. Fabricating. Dodging. Pussyfooting. Deceiving. Bald-faced lying. These are all ways to evade the truth. Nor do liars only deceive others. They often deceive themselves as well. How much reality can most of us bear about ourselves if that reality is unattractive, at best, or downright ugly. I've known selfish people who really believe themselves to be the most generous people walking the face of the earth. I've known both educated and uneducated people who claim to have answers for everything, and never lack an opinion about things of which they are more or less totally ignorant. "To thine own self be true and thou canst not then be false to any man," says Polonius to his son Laertes in Shakespeare's *Hamlet*. Truth begins at home and extends from the heart to everyone around you. Truth is precious. It demands enormous respect. To be sure, there are times when it must be expressed in a forthright, even confrontational, way and other times when it's best handled with great tact and delicacy. But truth must always be used with integrity, for, as the old adage goes, it is the truth that makes us free, and one with the angels.

TALKING THINGS OUT

I am always amazed that so many people make light of what's come to be known as "talk therapy." People who don't understand its value ridicule it. Third party insurance reimbursers pay less for it than one would pay to have a plumber repair a leaky pipe. Even doctors, who should know better, sometimes snicker when reference is made to it. Yet it has been convincingly shown to make a tremendous difference in many people's lives, when it is competently and proficiently carried out.

Communications are the heart's blood of psychotherapy. Having practiced both psychological and biological psychiatry for years, I recognize that many of the elements that enter into successful communication between doctor and patient can be learned and used in our communications with everybody.

Let's begin with trust. Beyond telling the truth, communication relies on trusting that the person with whom you are communicating isn't out to hurt you. If you tell someone something confidential, you must be able to trust that he or she will keep it to themselves. You also have to trust that the person you're speaking with isn't trying to manipulate you or deny you the right to your own perspective, even if presently it's a faulty one, which in due time will hopefully yield to correction.

Then there's taking the time to really understand what each other is trying to communicate. This requires patience, and listening, and more listening, and honest inquiry. Angels have the advantage of always being clear in what they say. We humans unfortunately don't. So, often it's a struggle to express ourselves and to comprehend the real meaning of what another person is saying. Between parents and adolescents and between husbands and wives there's a great tendency for the listener to "jump the gun," to presume that he or she knows what the speaker is expressing before the speaker has an opportunity to explain.

Keep in mind that communicating involves emotions and feelings as well as ideas. This is what can make it so difficult for us humans. Positive emotions such as love and joy and laughter are easy to take. But anger's another matter. I've seen plenty of couples who are furious with one another. Sometimes they have trouble putting their feelings into words. Sometimes they don't seem able to stop. I remember one patient who used to scream so loudly at her husband that my secretary once buzzed me on the intercom to be sure I was all right.

Before any meaningful communication can take place, you have to achieve some degree of calmness. You can be direct. You can say, "Please try to lower your voice," or, "I know how angry you are, but try to take a deep breath and let yourself quiet down, so we can find out what you're really so angry about." Or you can let it run its course, maintaining a cool head all the while and not doing anything to aggravate an already explosive situation.

I've seen angry parents and their teenage sons and daughters too. More often than not, the youngster's anger is controlled and is expressed as silence, while his or her parents can barely contain their frustration. It's as if they want to shout at the adolescent but don't dare to, not in front of a stranger, at any rate. Or sometimes their frustration is the expression of fear and futility over their own failed attempts to communicate with someone they really care about.

What's called for is patience, a call for honesty, helping everyone appreciate that whatever the problems may be, they're best resolved by the simple act of talking them out.

Angel-like qualities are invaluable in these difficult situations, most of all the quiet assurance that the real goal is the genuine well-being of all concerned. When parents *honestly* want only the best for themselves and their youngsters, and youngsters *honestly* want only the best for themselves and their parents, and spouses *honestly* want only the best for each other, *and everyone involved knows that this is so*, they will have gone a long way toward maintaining good communications and restoring them should they be lost.

COMMUNICATING WITHOUT WORDS

Of course, we communicate without words too, with gestures, with how we position our bodies, with the look in our eyes, with the expression on our faces. These nonverbal cues can help get our messages across, or they may betray the fact that we are lying. When we are telling the truth but our appearance and actions seem to disagree with our words, it can be very confusing indeed, and it certainly doesn't inspire trust. So it's important to make every effort to achieve harmony between what you say, what your body seems to be communicating, and what your overall behavior reflects. In other words, if you love someone, look as though you mean it when you say "I love you," and act as if your love for him or her is real (actions speak louder than words). Don't lead a selfish life that contradicts everything you've said and may well suggest that you've been lying even to yourself.

THE RIGHT KIND OF SMILE

Even your smile can serve you or betray you. Did you know that one kind of smile may make people distrust you, even if you are as trustworthy as an angel, while another warms hearts, radiates sincerity, and actually promotes your own sense of well-being?

A hundred years ago the French neurologist G. B. Duchenne, observed that there was more than one way to smile. But only one smile went along with positive emotions such as love or joy. It became known as the Duchenne smile, which was characterized by an upward pulling of the corners of the lip and, at the same time, a pulling of the skin above and below the eyes toward the orbits themselves. The cheeks are pulled up. The skin below the eyes bulges slightly. The lower eyelid moves up. Crow-feet wrinkles may appear at the outer corner of the eye socket. The skin above the eye is pulled slightly down and in, and the eyebrows move down ever so slightly.

Apparently there are two distinct neural pathways mediating facial expression, each originating in a different part of the brain. One responds to will. The other is involuntary, activated by spontaneous emotions. A Duchenne smile is smooth. It lasts about half a second to five seconds. If you watch a movie that elicits positive emotions, the number of your Duchenne smiles increases, whereas watching violent films that elicit negative emotions, such as anger or fear, reduces your number of such smiles.

With the Duchenne smile, other people will judge you to be more pleasant, outgoing, likable, sincere, honest, and genuine. Unfortunately, about 20 percent of people can fake this smile, so it's not an absolute guarantee of friendliness or trustworthiness.

It's hardly my purpose to encourage duplicity. But if you are an honest person who wishes others well, why not practice the Duchenne smile to be more effective in communicating how you think and feel? Here's how you can do it. Look into a mirror. Now raise your cheeks. Part your lips and let the corners come up. Squinting or lightly closing your eyes may help. You're using the right muscles when you do that. Now do it again, without closing your eyes. Add a smile. Hold that pose for at least twenty seconds. There, you've got it. Practice it to make it a habitual part of your communication style.

THE WILL TO COMMUNICATE KNOWINGLY AND WITH LOVE

Just how important it is to develop effective communication styles is readily seen by citing a few of the dire consequences of failing to communicate. Crippled communication styles in parents usually produce crippled children. Faulty communications are the icebergs that sink many marriages. They can cost jobs or block advancement at work and can lead to a wide array of frustrating events, from arguing with a credit card company's customer representative to missing out forever on some of life's best opportunities.

One of my prime responsibilities as a psychiatrist is to communicate effectively with my patients and to help them learn how to communicate more effectively in their own lives. One of my responsibilities as a human being is to do this everywhere else as well. This calls for *will* (I must want to communicate successfully); *intellect* (I must always be looking for ways to improve my skills); and *love* (I must care enough for others to want to reach out to them).

This brings us back to angels. Whether they're addressing Moses in Egypt or Mary in Nazareth, their messages are purposeful. If they do engage in idle pleasantries, they appear to restrict such behavior to their interplay with other angels. Their messages are useful. They are lucid. Above all, they are honest. It's the truth.

The form their communication takes is important too. Their messages are delivered in such a way as to be reassuring and comforting. . .unless, of course, they are meant to terrify, threatening punishment and oblivion, as in the case of Sodom and Gomorrah. Don't make the mistake of thinking that angels are always pussycats.

And keep in mind that we human beings are not the only concern of angels. They are busy doing other things too, such as singing and praying to God.

THE MAGIC OF MUSIC

Music is also a form of communication.

Dr. Alfred Tomatis is a French physician whose research has helped establish the healing and creative powers of sound and music in general and of the "Mozart effect" in particular. He suggested that listening to Mozart's music affects the brain in such a way as to enhance the listener's ability to perform spatial and temporal tasks, improve concentration, and heighten the ability to make intuitive leaps. The secret to the power of Mozart's music may be its purity and simplicity.

We all know that sound can be soothing, such as the sound of a human voice. I have a friend whose voice has the most calming and joyous effect when I hear it, and it often doesn't seem to matter what she is talking about. Reading poetry aloud can speak directly to our hearts, physically as well as emotionally, sharing as it does many of the tonalities and rhythms of music. In fact, the effective use of language is itself a form of music.

Don Campbell titled the preface (called overture) to his book *The Mozart Effect*, "The Speech of Angels and Atoms." He writes, "In an instant, music can uplift our soul. It awakens within us the spirit of prayer, compassion, and love. It clears our minds. . .[it] is a holy place. . .It is the primal breath of creation itself, the speech of angels and atoms, the stuff of which life and dreams, souls and stars are ultimately fashioned."

Angels are known for their singing, which may also reinforce their already superior intelligence. Maybe they listen to Mozart. Or perhaps they inspired Mozart in the first place. I'd be very curious to hear what choirs of angels sound like. Some day I hope I shall. In the meantime, I'll have to settle for Mozart, Rachmaninoff, Grieg, Frank Sinatra, and the Beatles.

Why do angels sing? Because they like to, I suppose. But most of all in praise of God. Singing is a form of prayer.

PRAYER

Humans pray with song too—"Amazing Grace," "Rock of Ages," Gregorian chant. But we can pray in simpler ways as well, and isn't prayer a form of long-distance communication?

I'm not the least bit hesitant to suggest to patients who believe in prayer to pray over the dilemmas they face. I'd be foolish not to. And I tell them that in my own experience, prayers are always answered, although not necessarily as we might expect them to be. You have to be careful what you pray for.

Some years ago I was on a panel with Dr. Bernie S. Siegal, author of the best-selling book *Love, Medicine and Miracles.* He had just finished speaking about the power of prayer to help people recover from their illnesses. The time for questions arrived. "Dr. Siegal," I asked, "do you think, when people pray, that someone up there is listening?" He just smiled. I'm still not quite sure what he believes, but I do know he firmly believes in praying, whether you're a marine in a foxhole, or about to be wheeled into the operating room at Massachusetts General Hospital.

Here's a simple structure for prayer:

"I worship you, God.
"I'm really sorry for any ways in which I may have failed you."
"Thanks for all you've done for me."
"I love you."
"Please help others."
"Please help me."

GUIDELINES FOR MODELING OURSELVES AFTER ANGELS

Communicating

- Make a habit of telling the truth. Be a person others can trust.

- Enjoy the spontaneity of conversation. You don't have to think about everything you say before you say it if you have already developed a habit of speaking affirmatively and with good will.

- Give careful thought to what and how you intend to say something if it's something really important or if you're concerned about how someone else will react to it.

- Be prepared to explain yourself, without impatience, if what you've said doesn't seem to have been understood.

- Listen, and be sure you understand what's being said to you.

- Find a vocabulary with which to express your emotions such as joy, fear, and anger. Children often express their feelings primarily through their behavior. As they grow up, one of their primary tasks as adolescents is to learn how to do so verbally rather than by what's called acting out—bullying other kids in the school yard, stealing costume jewelry in a department store, refusing to study for exams and getting Fs—instead of being able to voice their frustrations in constructive ways. Many adults also have trouble putting their emotions into words. If you have trouble in your marriage, facing up to it and talking it out is much better than involving yourself in a clandestine affair or just refusing to communicate at all. If you're having difficulties at work, speaking about them in search of solutions beats coming home and pounding the wall with your fists, or engaging in what's called passive-aggressive behavior, like frequently coming in late, provoking your boss, or sneaking cigarettes in the washroom of a smoke-free workplace.

- Learn to appreciate the power and beauty of language. It took thousands of years for language to evolve to the point that Shakespeare could write *Romeo and Juliet* or Kenneth Grahame *The Wind in the Willows*. Winston Churchill's eloquence was one of the Allies' most potent weapons in World War II, even as Adolph Hitler's mesmerizing rhetoric persuasively spewed out his messages of evil. Even Humphrey Bogart's line at the end of the film *Casablanca*, "Here's looking at you, kid," has its own down-to-earth dignity. This is not to imply that we must become masters of the art. But the more you appreciate what a wonderful gift language is, the more likely you'll be to use it effectively and avoid descending to the lowest common denominator, interrupting every other sentence with four-letter vulgarities.

- Accentuate the positive. Observe the old adage that if you don't have something good to say, don't say anything. Praise behavior that deserves praise. Critique when it's appropriate for you to do so, but don't engage in destructive criticism or be an eager messenger of defamation.

- Pay attention to what you communicate nonverbally, and be sure your stance, gestures, and overall behavior are consistent with your words. And learn to smile, since smiling goes a long way toward making everyone comfortable, including yourself.

- Pray. Pray silently. Pray aloud. Pray when you're in trouble. Pray when you're not. Pray alone. Pray with others. Pray the prayers given us to pray, the Psalms of David, the Lord's Prayer. Pray casual prayers that you've made up yourself. Make your work a prayer. Make your relationships with others a prayer. Make your life a prayer.

REILLY
And now we are ready to proceed with the
libation

ALEX
The words for the building of the hearth

REILLY
Let them build the hearth
Under the protection of the stars

ALEX
Let them place a chair each side of it

JULIA
May the holy ones watch over the roof,
May the Moon herself influence the bed.

ALEX
The words for those who go upon a journey

REILLY
Protector of travelers
Bless the road

ALEX
Watch over her in the desert
Watch over her in the mountain
Watch over her in the labyrinth
Watch over her by the quicksand

JULIA
Protect her from the Voices
Protect her from the Visions
Protect her from the tumult
Protect her in the silence

REILLY
There is one for whom the words cannot
be spoken

ALEX
They cannot be spoken yet.

JULIA
You mean Peter Quilpe.

REILLY
He has not come to where the words are
valid

JULIA
Shall we ever speak them?

ALEX
Others, perhaps, will speak them.
You know, I have connections—even in
California.

The Cocktail Party
T. S. ELIOT

X

THE FIFTH STRENGTH

A Mission to Guide and Protect

In which you will become more familiar with the responsibilities of crossing guards, seat belt installers, emergency rescue workers, and parents

WHERE ARE YOU HEADED?

In the film *The Edge*, Charles, played by Anthony Hopkins, saves himself by following a few very rudimentary guidelines in a book on finding one's way out of any wilderness. He would have saved his two companions as well, if one had not been dismembered by a bear and the other had not died from injuries sustained when he fell into a pit. Angels are known to have a remarkable sense of direction, which they often use on our behalf. If you think of people modeling themselves after angels, Charles was working overtime, engaged in one of the routine jobs that angels do, to lead and guide.

I am known in my family for having a good sense of direction. Whenever we get lost while driving and don't have the benefit of a map, I seem to have an instinct for knowing which way to go. Unlike that of angels, however, mine is fallible, and we occasionally end up pulling into the nearest gas station to get our bearings.

What is true for driving your car cross-country or traveling in a foreign land is no less true for your entire life. "Where am I going?" is a question most of us ask at various stages of life. Helping us answer this question is what guardian angels do, sometimes by whispering softly in our ears, sometimes by placing opportunity in our path, like a roadsign that we can choose to follow or not. Responding to angel messages is not obligatory. The choice is always yours.

Just think of the countless ways in which every one of us is called upon to exert leadership. Parents lead their children. Teachers lead their students. Priests, ministers, and rabbis lead the members of their congregations. Supervisors lead those who work under them, from the top of the organization down. Generals, admirals, staff sergeants, boatswain's mates; boy scout leaders and Little League coaches; vocational guidance counselors; politicians and statespersons—in every one of these arenas, we have the chance to become more angel-like in our performance.

MOM AND DAD

There is probably no more important leadership post than that of parent. A great deal more goes into bringing up children than providing them with a roof over their heads and three square meals a day. Providing love goes without saying, as does performing the mundane, tedious chores, especially during the first couple of years of life. Parental leadership begins with an infant's first breath, if not earlier, back to the moment that the decision to have a child was made. Now, I'm not a believer in the blank-slate theory of personality, which holds that we are nothing more than products of our environments. I think we all come into this world with traits of our own, in part determined by genetics, but in part a reflection of every human being's singular individuality. Nonetheless, we are profoundly affected by what happens to us during our formative years.

Your leadership style as a parent derives from several sources. The model your parents provided you with is one source. You may choose to embrace it, modify it, or reject it altogether in favor of an approach to parenting that is all your own. Of course, you can't escape the model entirely. It can creep in on you when you least expect it, which may be good or bad, depending on what kind of model it was.

Then there are the conscious choices you make about the sort of parent you want to be. Maybe you don't want your children to be too materialistic, so, unlike other parents in your neighborhood, you don't want to buy them everything they desire. Of course, you'll have to explain this to them in terms they can understand, so they don't feel deprived because their playmates' rooms are awash with toys and clothes and trinkets of every sort. Or maybe you intelligently choose to refrain from physical punishment, knowing that a serious look is often all that's required to get your message across. Or perhaps you choose to resist their pleading to watch television hour after hour, encouraging them to use their time more fruitfully instead. Then, too there are the popular books on child rearing by people such as Benjamin Spock and T. Berry Brazelton, which you read to find out more about what to expect of a two-year-old or a four-year-old, or just for general guidance.

The parent who wants to follow in the footsteps of angels will help each child develop his or her intellect, will, and spirituality. There are other things to look after, as well, that don't have much of a bearing on angel behavior, like toilet training, nutrition, or teaching a youngster how to ride a bike. But foremost in a parent's mind should be teaching one's child to know *how to know*—to experience the joy of discovery. When one of my sons was less than two years old, we put signs all around his room identifying objects with written names: bed, dresser, table, lamp, book, window, door, and the like. He had fun with it and learned to read well ahead of many children his age. I also remember playing games with my children, such as assembling a cardboard grocery store and pretending to be shopkeeper and customer for an hour at a time. Once they began school, we never failed to praise them for work well done, something I learned the importance of from my own upbringing.

I recall that when one of my daughters was four, she started a preschool program a block away from home. I walked her there in the mornings, holding her hand. Sometimes she would let go of my hand when we arrived and go upstairs one flight to her classroom by herself. Other times she wouldn't let go, pulling me with her, signaling that she wanted me to walk up too and maybe even stay there for a while. I let her make the choice, respecting her desire for independence as well as her need to still be the little girl. I have no doubt it strengthened her will.

The context of the guidance a parent gives changes with the years. One morning you wake up and suddenly your little girl or boy is practically an adult. You are still very much needed, even if this would-be grown up doesn't like the idea very much. Diplomatically make it known that you're always *available* to offer advice about relationships, friends, boyfriends and girlfriends, sex, college admissions, and the direction they will take in their work and careers. Keep in mind that you still know a lot they don't know, even if they think they do. The challenge now is to maintain channels of communication (which you can learn something about from angels) and to know how to mix setting limits (which they absolutely require) with a genuine respect for their urge toward independence. Acknowledge the fact that you may be able to learn something from them. And do all this in the spirit of love, with a willingness to forgive, and wish everyone well.

Wishing everyone well has never been a more important need, considering how many children are raised in single-parent homes. Divorced parents too often hold onto an anger and disdain for one another that may have led to the divorce in the first place. Unforgiving, they speak and behave in derogatory ways toward each other, sometimes for years. And the primary victims of their hate are their children. How much more fruitful and angel-like it would be for divorced mothers and fathers to acknowledge that their children have two parents whom they must respect in order to get on with their own lives in a healthy way.

MINISTERS, TEACHERS, AND MARINE CORPS CAPTAINS

Leadership in the family is only the beginning of your opportunities to learn from the angels how to guide. No matter what profession you are in or at what level of an organization you find yourself, you are going to be called upon to be a model for others, helping them to do their jobs more effectively, motivating them to use their talents and become the best they can be at what they do. If you're a minister, you're expected to inspire people to lead virtuous lives. If you're a plant manager, you're expected to instill a spirit of dedication to excellence on the assembly line. If you're a teacher, you're expected to excite your pupils in the pursuit of knowledge. If you're a marine captain, you may have to give your troops the will to win, and a willingness to die, if necessary, in the struggle for victory.

A captain of marines can learn as much from angels as rehabilitation therapists helping the wounded to walk again can learn. *Don't make the mistake of thinking of angels as softies. They're not. They're tough as any soldier, tougher maybe.* But good angels—and those are the ones I'm obviously describing—are committed to what is genuinely good. You can hardly imagine angels as leaders waving their arms in the air and directing a group of skiers toward a patch of thin ice that will collapse under their weight and plunge them hundreds of feet into a deep crevasse to their deaths.

We too must be concerned about the direction in which we are leading those with whom we live and work and play. The mission of any group or organization of which you are in charge should be something worthwhile and consistent with the highest purposes of being human. This doesn't mean you have to quit being the manager of an automobile showroom and run off to become a social worker in Central America. It means you should be selling cars that are as safe as possible to drive and will hold up reasonably well, asking a fair price, dealing honestly with your customers, and servicing them properly after they've purchased an automobile from you. If you're not happy with the quality of your product, let the manufacturer know and keep after them to do something about it.

If you're the governor of a state, you are serving *all* the people, and it's your job to create an environment that will afford everyone a chance for a decent life; you have to find ways to balance fairly but effectively the divergent interests that are always at play in a democratic society. If you're the coach of a team you have to excite your players to give it their all, without unfair tactics or energizing drugs. Companies spend hundreds of millions of dollars on motivational training, especially on behalf of their sales force. Everyone knows how important effective leadership is. The angel's question remains: leadership toward what end?

EVERYONE SHOULD BE A MENTOR

Mentoring is a vital form of guidance. It may be one of the most angel-like activities that we all have the chance to pursue. A mentor is someone who helps someone else grow to his or her potential. The direction and encouragement a mentor gives is based on a genuine understanding of who and what someone is now, and what he or she can become. It's motivated by altruism. It involves giving another person time and thought, and sharing one's own experiences and wisdom with that person. I certainly owe much to my own mentors over the years of my apprenticeship in life. I remember a very special teacher, when I was in the eighth grade, encouraging me to take high school scholarship examinations and providing me with a time and place to prepare for them during the school day. There was a professor at college who guided me as I became proficient in debating and public speaking. He also impressed upon me the importance of justice in race relations, on one occasion arranging for me to give a talk on why it was essential to provide more employment opportunities for black workers to a group of not-very-open-minded members of a local labor union.

I won't go on to list all my mentors, except to say that my own parents were perhaps my most significant ones. That's where you can certainly begin, if you have children: taking a serious interest in their studies; urging them to develop their strengths, whether at the computer or the piano, or on the athletic field; listening to their hopes and ambitions and helping them find a meaningful place for the themselves in the world; reminding them, as much through your own behavior as anything else, of the critical importance of faith and the life of the spirit.

You can do the same where you work, mentoring talented young people under your supervision. You can be a mentor to your spouse, who may be in need of encouragement and direction. If you're a teacher, mentoring goes with the job. In fact, there are innumerable opportunities to assume the angel-like responsibility of mentoring, from counseling someone who's recently widowed, to coaching a Little League baseball team, to being a Big Brother or Big Sister to a youngster who desperately needs your friendship.

THE ETHICS OF LEADERSHIP

Leadership can carry with it considerable power over others. Those who follow you trust you. Don't betray that trust. Teachers and students, doctors with their patients, lawyers with their clients, have the potential for great good and great harm.

The widespread concern over ethics today has been spurred on by the discovery of serious violations of trust in the form of seduction, theft, betrayal, incompetence. Hardly a day goes by without a headline story in the newspaper: A high school teacher in her thirties becomes pregnant by one of her pupils. A well-known psychiatrist is accused of using sedatives to put his female patients to sleep, and then, raping them. An attorney is jailed for embezzling money from an estate he's been entrusted to manage. A radio personality bilks thousands of elderly people out of their life savings. Accounts of child abuse and abuse of the elderly never seem to end. And these incidents are only the ones we hear about.

People who depend on you can often be quite vulnerable, frightened, dependent, mesmerized, idolizing, enchanted. (Of course, they can also tempt you to do things that are out of line.) Laws by themselves are not enough to contain such behavior. What we all need is *great faith in and fear of* God and His angels, and the will to emulate their virtues. *They are always watching us*, in everything we think and do. In spite of their basic desire to be helpful, angels are not creatures to be taken too lightly or to offend.

JOINING THE RESCUE TEAM

Saving people from peril is what we hear most about when we're told of angel encounters. When I was speaking with a close friend of mine, Norman, about this book, he suddenly recalled what may have been two angel interventions in his life. "I used to think of it as ESP [extra-sensory perception]," he said. "But now that we're talking about angels, maybe. . . ."

Norman was a navy fighter pilot in the Second World War. During training exercises at Pensacola, Florida, a gunnery practice run involved a group of five planes, one at a time, shooting at a moving target being towed behind a sixth member of the squadron. It was Norman's turn to split off from the formation at 6,000 feet and dive down toward the sleeve 2,000 feet below, machine guns roaring. Quickly he was below the target. It was time to pull up out of his dive. Just before doing so, however, pilots routinely blacked out, but they were so well trained that they would automatically point the

plane upward, even before fully regaining consciousness. Norman did so. Suddenly, as if in a daze, he caught
sight of another plane, no more than thirty feet in front
of him. He could even make out its propeller. The next
pilot who was to make the run hadn't waited the full
sixty seconds he was supposed to. He had begun his dive
prematurely. There he was, coming in on the target as
Norman was pulling up. A midair collision seemed
inevitable. With seconds to spare, Norman instinctive-
ly put the nose of his plane down and dove toward the
water 4,000 feet below before leveling off. It was not
until he had landed at the base that the full impact of
the experience struck him, and he felt the terror of it.

"I can't explain what happened," he told me. "We
should have been killed. Was it an angel intervention?"

His next recollection involved driving with his two
young sons along a two-lane highway north of New
York. They'd been to a party, but Norman had had
nothing to drink and he was not fatigued. It was
evening and beginning to get dark. Suddenly, with neither rhyme nor reason, he pulled off the road onto the
shoulder and stopped his car. Seconds later, two cars
rounded a curve up ahead and plummeted toward him.
One was passing the other. Their headlights momen-
tarily blinded him. As they roared past he realized that
if he had not pulled off the road, he and his sons would
undoubtedly have been seriously injured or killed.

"Might well have been angels all," this very
bright, worldly-wise, and certainly spiritual friend of
mine suggested, looking more than a little pleased by
the thought.

We are all protectors, whether you're a parent
telling your children to fasten their safety belts or

wear a life-jacket in the boat, or a homeowner lock-
ing the windows and doors at night so prowlers can't
get into your home. On more than one occasion, you
may find yourself standing up for friends when others
attack them unfairly. Or you may find yourself saving
them from themselves, as when you encourage them
to give up smoking or cut back on their drinking or
look after their health or pay more serious attention
to their work lest they lose their jobs. We all serve as
crossing guards.

Of course, maybe you really do protect people
professionally. Maybe you are a policeman, an FBI
agent, an officer in the army, a fireman, or a member
of an emergency rescue team. If so, have you ever
thought of the fact that you walk in the footsteps of
angels? Or rather, you can walk that way if you choose
to. Doing so will help you resist any temptations to
abuse your authority or to be brutal in your dealings
with people. Power (which sometimes involves carrying a gun) is morally neutral. It's how you use that
power that counts. You must act, as angels do, firmly,
decisively when you're called on to protect others or
yourself.

Ask yourself who needs your protection? Maybe
you're a lawyer and your client faces serious charges
or is going through a divorce. Or you're a psychiatrist
whose patient is a threat to himself or others. As a
physician you have an obligation to prevent people
from injuring themselves, and that can mean taking
away their freedom for a while through a process
called commitment. And if a patient has targeted a
person for serious injury or even murder, doctors are
obliged by law—it's called the Tarasoff decision—to

inform the potential victim and the police, ordinary rules of professional confidentiality not withstanding. Of course, the best way for physicians to help keep their patients from self-injury or suicide is by creating a strong, positive, trusting relationship with them that affords a sense of security, and by treating them skillfully and effectively.

Maybe you're an accountant with a client who needs to be protected in an audit with the IRS. Perhaps you're the child of an aging parent, no longer strong and independent, who needs your care and attention. You may be a manufacturer of automobiles, whose job it is to provide your customers with the safest car you can produce, or the manager of a pharmaceutical company, and it's up to you to see that any drug you plan to introduce is both safe and effective before you release it. Of course, it's obvious that our environment is desperately in need of protection. You can send money to organizations that are working to prevent the further destruction of rain forests, and you can stop throwing litter in rivers and along the road.

CAVEATS FOR WOULD-BE HEROES

There's an old adage that fools rush in where angels fear to tread. In your earnest desire to save and protect, don't try to exceed your limitations. You don't have to swim half a mile out to sea to rescue someone who's in trouble if you're not a strong swimmer. Nor need you rush into a flaming building unless you happen to be a fireman. There are exceptional moments, however, instances of genuine heroism, when one person risks his or her life to save another. Whatever awards we give such heroes, whether it's coverage on the nightly news or the Congressional Medal of Honor, no doubt the angels themselves rejoice that a human being could be so like them.

You can, however, be *too* protective. Overprotecting children, as most of us appreciate—not letting them take a few risks, keeping them 100 percent out of harm's way—can cripple their sense of self-confidence. Becoming self-reliant is part of growing up; it can be learned only through experience.

Nor should you become locked into a destructive relationship as a codependent. In their often sincere efforts to be helpful to someone in desperate need, certain people naively play into that need in such a way as to encourage its continuation and eat away at their own self-respect. Professionals see this most commonly among friends and families of substance abusers. But the risk exists in other situations too. Certain people thrive on creating one crisis after another, hoping you will save them every time, and you may feel compelled to do just that. Situations like this can be pretty complicated, and if you think you're trapped in one, you would do well to seek professional advice and guidance.

You should also protect other people from yourself, being a locksmith to the heart and soul as well as to the body, wishing others well and being steady and consistent in your behavior toward them. Few situations are more imprisoning than to be caught in a relationship with someone who continually delivers mixed messages, such as "I love you, but I can't commit myself." On one side of this interaction, you can protect another person by courageously and honestly coming to terms with your own ambivalence and choosing to resolve it, either in the direction of commitment or of separation. On the other side, if you can't persuade the ambivalent person with whom you are involved to make such a choice, you must escape. To get away, you may require the help of an angel, or of a human being striving to be angel-like. And maybe you can be the angel who helps a friend find his or her way back to freedom and a chance to find a new love relationship that promises genuine harmony.

ANGELS IN THE SNOW

When I told a patient of mine whom I have known, on and off, for more than thirty years that I was writing about angels, he smiled. I knew he did not believe in angels, or in God for that matter, although he was open-minded enough to allow the possibility of both. Then suddenly he looked startled. "I just remembered something that happened to me years ago, when I was skiing in Switzerland," he said. "I had left the main trail. Feeling a bit adventurous, I suppose. I thought could get back down the slopes more quickly that way. But I fell and sprained my ankle. It was late in the afternoon, and bitter cold. I was really scared. I had little hope that the ski patrol would find me so far off the regular paths. It was getting dark. I was certain I'd freeze to death up there, all alone. And then, all of a sudden, at the top of the slope, I could see two figures skiing steadily toward me. As they came closer, I could see their uniforms. I knew I'd be rescued."

I asked him if they said anything to him.

"Only that I'd been foolish. Nothing else that I can remember. They just went about putting me on a sled and towing me downhill, back to the village and the first-aid station. Funny. Even though they pulled me over bumps and small crevices, it was a strangely smooth ride."

"What happened when you got back to the village?"

"Nothing special. They took off. I never saw them again."

"Did you get their names?"

"Yes, but I don't remember." He smiled again. "Maybe they were angels, or members of the ski patrol sent to help me by angels."

"But you don't believe in God or angels. Why would they bother to help you?" I asked jokingly.

He laughed. "Maybe because I had a doctor who did believe."

GUIDELINES FOR MODELING OURSELVES AFTER ANGELS

To Guide and Protect

- Identify your leadership opportunities and responsibilities. Some careers obviously involve protecting and rescuing, such as being a policeman or a fireman. In other careers, the mission to guide and protect may be less obvious but no less real. You may be a teacher, or a doctor, or a lawyer. You may be a parent. You may be a protector of trees.

- Make out a list of those who need your guidance and protection, and don't forget aging parents and friends who are going through terrible crises in their lives.

- If you're a parent, raise your children the way all children deserve to be raised. That means not only attending to their physical needs but giving them love and inspiration. Keep in mind that they will use you as a model, so be the kind of model that will allow them to grow up to be successful human beings. Help them cultivate their talents. Encourage them to do well in whatever they choose to do. Offer them spiritual leadership, especially by the values you hold and the examples you present. Teach them how to pray. And, now and then, remind them of angels.

- Whether you're a teacher, a minister, a business manager, or a captain of marines, instill a spirit of virtue and a dedication to excellence in all those who look to you for direction.

- Be a mentor. Make yourself available—and let them know you're available—to your children, your spouse, your friends, the people with whom you work, the students you teach, to whomever it seems appropriate, to offer guidance and advice that can help them develop their abilities to their fullest and embrace the kind of values that will assure them a virtuous and meaningful journey through life.

- Don't rush in where angels fear to tread. In your efforts to help others, don't overprotect them or go beyond your own limitations. Make no promises on which you cannot deliver. And don't get embroiled in destructive relationships with people who, in their own determined effort to drown themselves, seem insistent that those who reach out to help them drown as well. Be careful about making citizens' arrests, and leave the tough cases to the professionals.

- Go strictly by the book. Always observe the rules of moral behavior. If you're a policeman, this means no more Rodney Kings. Don't drink when driving. And never take advantage of those who, in their time of weakness, turn to you for help, or whose admiration for you makes them especially susceptible to your will.

- Know where you're leading everyone, and be sure it's a place worth going to, one pleasing to the unseen angels who will be with you all the way.

When a flood of sick came in she was on her feet all day. She was known to spend eight hours on her knees dressing wounds, and she would work the clock round. She never let a man she had tended die alone. She estimated that during that winter she witnessed 2,000 deaths. There was never a severe case that escaped her notice. She did her rounds every night carrying her lantern which she would set down before she bent down over any of the patients. 'What a comfort it was to see her pass even,' wrote a soldier. 'She would speak to one, and nod and smile to as many more; but she could not do it all you know. We lay there by hundreds; but we could kiss her shadow as it fell and lay our heads on the pillow again content'.

Florence Nightengale:
The Young Heroine in Creative Malady
Sir George Pickering

XI

THE SIXTH STRENGTH
Healing and Helping

*For those who want to give a helping hand and those
who sometimes hope for miracles*

RAPHAEL IS said to be the angel of healing, but I'm
sure he has plenty of help from the rest of the angels
and could use some from us as well. Perhaps you may be
asking, What can I do? I'm not trained to be a doctor or
nurse, or even a psychotherapist. I don't have any special healing powers. I even get sick at the sight of blood.
How can I be a healer?

If that's the way you think, you need to broaden
your definition of healing, because there's much more
to helping others overcome sickness of the mind, the
body, and the soul than performing surgery or prescrib-
ing medication.

We doctors know that a patient's attitude can seriously affect the outcome of his or her illness. I remember being called in consultation to evaluate a forty-

something-year-old woman who was about to undergo major surgery for a bleeding ulcer (before the days when we recognized that ulcers were caused by bacteria and could be treated with drugs to reduce acidity and with antibiotics to kill off the infection). After talking with her, I concluded that she was very depressed and didn't really want to live. I told the surgeons and suggested they delay the operation. But they felt they had to go ahead with it, because she was at serious risk of dying if they didn't. The patient never made it through the surgery. The surgeons could offer no explanation for her sudden death. I could. I believe she willed herself to die. I learned what a powerful force hope is in giving us the strength to overcome disease, disorders of the body such as a heart attack, and wounds of the heart such as betrayal by a loved one.

So, while only a small number of us will train to be professionals, all of us can develop angel-like skills to help others overcome the weaknesses to which flesh is heir and the profound heartaches that few of us escape in the course of our lives.

There are five angel attributes that we can cultivate to help us achieve this goal.

- Inspiring hope

- Comforting and supporting

- Restoring morale to help one regain command of one's life

- Empathizing

- Forgiving

INSPIRING HOPE

Hope is an optimistic attitude toward the future: I will get better. I will get a good job. I will find a new love.

Archibald Rutledge wrote a poem about hope that I read when I was in the navy. I was eighteen years old. At eighteen you're supposed to see the whole world opening up to you. You're excited by your prospects. You plan to live forever. Eighteen has a way of hoping for the moon. But that wasn't the way it was in those days. Too many young men were dying. There was too much horror, too much heartache. You had to hold on tight to your hope to get through it in one piece, win, and have done with it. Even if you weren't in immediate danger, you never knew when you might be.

I tore Rutledge's poem out of the *Saturday Evening Post*. I kept it in between the pages of a book I had with me and took it out from time to time to read these lines, because they simply made me feel better.

> O gallant Heart, defeated
> Now gazing toward the west,
> Where this day's splendor crumbles
> Disastrous and unblest,
> Look till the deathlike darkness
> By stars be glorified,
> Until you see another dream
> Beyond the dream that died.

It speaks to hope, which we all needed a lot of in those days, and which we all need a lot of every day of our lives.

Now, hope is a powerfully positive feeling. But it is not Pollyannish. True hope must be rooted in reality. Hoping for things that are inherently impossible can be an exercise in futility. Hope requires that there be at least a slim likelihood that what you hope for can be attained, even if that occasionally requires a miracle. Even if you are suffering with a fatal illness, you can be hopeful that the time remaining to you may be quality time, an opportunity to be with those you love, a chance to reassess life's meaning and pay some attention to your spiritual self.

There are a number of ways to reinforce hope. If you're dealing with a serious illness, carefully select your doctors, trust them, ask to be adequately informed about what's wrong with you and what's going to be done for you and of what your chances for recovery are. I find that patients who take an active role in their treatment have a greater sense of hope than those who don't.

Whatever your problems may be, don't give up. Keep on trying, until you find the answers you've been looking for, including ones that you may never have dreamed of when you began.

I know a young man who had lost his management position and had been out of work for nearly two years. He was married and had two children. His wife worked; she was their sole support. At the end of the day he'd frequently feel defeated, as if he'd never succeed in getting the kind of job he wanted, especially after a string of interviews with people who said they'd call him back but never did, and trip after trip to employment agencies and headhunters who told him they didn't have anything that quite fit his skills and experience. But every morning he'd get up and head for the phone and make some more calls. He kept going. He didn't give up hope. Then one day he answered his hundredth (or so) job ad in the *New York Times*. It wasn't quite what he had been looking for. It involved computer software sales. He knew something about software, but he'd never considered a sales job in his life, and he wasn't sure he could succeed at that. But he was desperate. Before his interview he went to the local library and took out half a dozen training videos on sales strategies so that he'd be better prepared. The sales manager who interviewed him was so impressed by his enterprise that he hired him on the spot. That was three years ago; since then he has become the company's star salesperson.

It's important to note that during this ordeal he had the continuing support of his wife, his family, his friends, and, whether he realized it or not, his guardian angel.

TO COMFORT AND SUPPORT

One of the easiest angel attributes to emulate is being there for others when they need you. Numerous studies have proven that *people who have people* have a significantly better chance of recovering from physical or mental illness, and staying well, than those who don't. My hunch is that you're already giving your support to a lot of people whom you know, giving them someone to talk with when they're upset, visiting them in hospitals or convalescent homes, spending the time with them that makes them feel loved and respected and *hopeful*.

The secret of being effectively supportive is knowing how to give encouragement. "You can do it. A step at a time. Easy now. Good. That's very good. Yes!" These words sound like a physical therapist helping a patient walk again after a serious accident. But they reflect an attitude that you can assume in helping anyone, anywhere, with anything. "You're going to do just fine in tomorrow's examination. You've put plenty of time into studying. Just read the questions carefully and take your time." Or, "Let's go over the numbers again and see how you might be able to get rid of some of these debts, and we'll make out a budget so you can turn things around once and for all."

A friend of mine, Alec, went through a shattering divorce some years ago. He was forty-three, had been married for nineteen years, and had three children. He hadn't wanted the divorce. But his wife was adamant in her refusal to reconcile. Alec felt utterly helpless— about saving his marriage, about building a life of his own afterward. His confidence hit rock bottom. He could barely attend to his work as an attorney. He was also very embarrassed by it all. Most of the friends Alec and his wife had were mutual, and they quickly dispersed. He was left with a handful of old friends, whom he hadn't seen all that often, including me.

I prepared a battle plan. I called up two of his other friends and worked out a strategy to help him reconstruct his life as quickly as possible. For that purpose we devised a series of helpful reassurances that we offered him as he seemed to need them: "You're better off without her, Alec." "Try not to have any hard feelings."

"Now you can really be yourself with your children."
"There are plenty of women out there when the time is
right." "Take it easy getting back to work. Let your part-
ners carry much of the load for a while."

We each had different assignments. One night a
week, one of us would have dinner with him. One
friend, Jeff, had a knack for finding apartments, so he
was given the task of helping Alec find a new place to
live. Another, Wallace, had a vast social life, so it was
his job to help Alec get back in the swing of things as
he felt ready.

One reason why there seem to be more angels
around these days may be because we so much need
their support. There's one angel-like activity that has
never before been so effective and so widespread: the
support group. There are support groups for breast cancer patients and families of Alzheimer victims, for people trying to give up smoking or alcohol, for patients
suffering with depression, for men with prostate cancer,
for victims of spousal abuse, and for people who were
adopted as children, to mention but a few. The thought
occurs to me: Where did the inspiration come from to
set these up?

BEING IN COMMAND OF YOUR LIFE

One of the goals of instilling hope and providing support
is to help us regain command over ourselves and our
lives when illness or adverse life events have made us
feel helpless. Helplessness can be viewed as a medical
emergency. Scientific studies have shown that feeling
helpless can wreak havoc with one's body as well as one's

mind. In prisoner-of-war camps, the soldiers who had the best chance for survival were those who continued to live within the framework of military protocol and stuck together throughout the ordeal. Life continued in an organized way, giving them a sense of being in command, even though this coherence extended no farther than the barbed wire fences that surrounded them.

People who are involved in a helpless struggle to get away from someone or some situation that is very troubling for them are often angry and frustrated, and they appear to be far more vulnerable to dying of heart attacks. People whose sense of helplessness stems from wanting someone or something desperately, while feeling that that person or thing is permanently unattainable, appear to be much more vulnerable to developing cancer. Helplessness, worry, and futility conspire to suppress the immune system and make us more likely to fall ill. That's probably why you and I are more likely to get a bad cold or the flu when we're under severe stress and strain.

Three of the most effective methods to get back in command again are *restoring morale* (said by psychiatrist Jerome Frank to be at the center of effective psychological therapy), *regaining perspective*, and *facing reality* for what it is, and no matter how bad things may be, accepting reality is the first step toward making things better.

In my own experience, one of the surest ways to restore morale is to find a rational explanation for what I am experiencing. I find that piecing things together, making a connection between some particular upsetting event and feelings that have been tearing me apart helps relieve the fear of not knowing what's happening to me or thinking I'm headed for a nervous breakdown.

Another way I restore my morale is to let go of any embarrassment I may feel for being so distressed. That may sound odd to those of you who cry easily and without self-consciousness. But many people have been brought up to feel that certain feelings, such as fear or depression, are a sign of weakness. So if we're frightened or depressed, it must mean we're weak, and that's something to be embarrassed about. It isn't, of course. Any good marine can tell you that not to be afraid going into battle is lunacy. You forge ahead, in spite of your fear. It's called courage. And if, when it's over, you cry for your buddies who have been killed, it's a sign of real manhood, and something to be proud of.

Perspective is often lost when you're feeling helpless and most vulnerable. It seems as if all time is now, and now is awful, and tomorrow doesn't look much better. If you find yourself feeling that way, stop and look back. Think of times when you were confident and happy and going somewhere you wanted to be going. You were successful then. You can be successful again. If you're wanting what you can never have, remember that you've been happy before without it. And if you feel helplessly trapped in a job or relationship that is making you feel frustrated and angry, say to yourself, "Anything is better than this!" and take your first step toward radically changing your attitude toward the people and situations that are upsetting you, or break away altogether.

Accepting—or helping someone else to accept—the predicament you're in for what it is is the necessary first step toward finding a cure. It's like making a diagnosis. A number of years ago, I was told that my prostate specific antigen test was higher than it should be. So I had a sonogram and a biopsy of my prostate. The five days that followed while I waited for the results, seemed interminable. I felt anxious, frightened, helpless. When I was told it was malignant, I felt a strange sense of relief. I'd rather it hadn't been. But now that I knew what I was dealing with, I went ahead to schedule surgery. And things seem to have been fine ever since.

Of course, I've seen patients who deny either the existence or consequences of their problems, usually at great risk. Denial is very common among alcoholics. It's also frequently seen among men and women who are involved in destructive relationships, especially when they are the destroyers. I've also known of two patients who refused to go along with their doctors' recommendations for treatment when they were diagnosed as having prostate cancer. They're both dead.

I KNOW HOW YOU MUST FEEL

The most powerful gift you can use to help someone feel better is empathy. The angel who comforted Jesus in the Garden of Gethsemane must have been empathic. It was not that he could have known from experience what Jesus was going through. He'd never been human. He'd never been God either, and many, such as myself, believe that Jesus is divine, the Son of God. All that the angel could fall back on to empathize with Jesus, then, was the angel's intellect, *knowing* what Jesus was experiencing and thereby offering him solace, as he had been bidden to do.

Angels also know that an angel appearance can be very scary, so they're careful to reassure those who witness one not to be afraid.

I've seen empathy work wonders, so often and so regularly that I am convinced of its central role in healing mind, body, and spirit. Empathy transcends compassion and sympathy. It involves experiencing vicariously what another person is experiencing for real. How can you really know what a person means when he or she tells you "I'm in love" if you've never been in love yourself? Even then, being in love may not have the same meaning for you as for him or her. How can you reach out empathically to comfort someone who is grieving unless you have known what it is to lose something or someone you cared for deeply? How can you share in the moment of victory—winning a significant promotion, a championship tennis tournament, a long and bloody legal battle—if you don't know what it is to win yourself?

Well, you can, *if* you value and emulate the example of *knowing* set by the angels. Life experience is the primary source of empathic power. But you can use your imagination, too, to richly and correctly feel what a particular human experience is like without necessarily having had to go through it. You can extrapolate from similar experiences. You may not know what it's like suddenly to lose a wife in her mid-forties of a heart attack. But you know how you felt when your mother or father or someone else close to you died, and from this you can draw conclusions about how the other person must feel.

Or you can draw on observation to make certain concepts and feelings part of your repertoire. You know what it's like to read a gripping novel or see a profoundly moving film. The intensity of your involvement in the plot and characters is a function of your capacity for vicarious experience. That involvement is a pretense, of course, and you know it's a pretense, but for the moment it can seem very real. And the memory of it can endure to help you empathize with real people going through similar moments in their lives.

THE GIFT OF FORGIVENESS

It has taken me years to come to appreciate the healing power of forgiveness. Few things corrode body and spirit as surely as old grievances, hurts, and resentments. The only remedy is forgiveness. And if you wonder whether angels forgive, you need only ask yourself how often you think your guardian angel has had to forgive you and stay there in your corner, mopping your brow and putting lotion on your injuries and getting you ready to go back for the next round.

There are several things that will help you understand the nature of forgiveness better. First, it does not involve denying the hurt you have suffered, whether real or exaggerated. Quite the contrary, the process requires you to look into yourself and admit to the sadness or anger that you feel. The next step entails looking at an incident in a different light, securing a deeper understanding of the motives of the person whose words or actions were the source of your pain. Were they intentional or unintentional? Were they the result of carelessness, insensitivity, stupidity, or downright meanness? Why do you think they behaved that way? Might you have done something to invite such behavior?

Once you have answered these questions, it's time to let go.

Each of us lets go in his or her own way. You might take a deep breath and resolve to stop thinking about your wounds. Or you might shake yourself all over, as if getting rid of a heavy burden you've been carrying. Or you might just say "I forgive you," quietly, to yourself.

Forgiveness is something you do *for your own sake*, not for the sake of others. They may never know whether you have forgiven them or not.

And it has nothing to do with whether you decide to continue a relationship as it's been, or to alter it as a result of what you've been through, or to end it once and for all.

Forgiving and moving on is called reconciliation. For example, you may decide that the person who hurt your feelings acted out of ignorance, and once you've forgiven him or her, you're ready to go on with the relationship, maybe after a little talk about what took place. Or you may decide that the person whom you had thought of as a friend never was a friend but acted out of selfishness, and that you're better off without him or her. Sometimes love deserves to prevail, and it does, with misunderstanding setting the stage for new understanding and forgiveness giving rise to greater intimacy and trust.

A FEW LAST WORDS FOR PROFESSIONAL HEALERS

All that I've said thus far applies to everyone, including those of us who are healers by profession—in our case, even more so. Doctors, nurses, therapists, and healers of all kinds have a special imperative to emulate angels.

Knowledge is the basis of sound medical care. We should learn all we can know about our work and make a habit of staying up-to-date and open to important new advances in medical science.

Wishing our patients well is a sine qua non of practice. It's why we are what we are. It's why we do what we do.

We must learn to *communicate* effectively with our patients and with our colleagues. Talking with patients, listening to them, answering their questions, taking the time to understand them, empathizing with them are all part of our *healing* mission.

And we ought to appreciate how lucky we are to be in a line of work that gives us the opportunity to help others as we do. The seal of New York Presbyterian Hospital, where I am a member of the staff, bears a drawing of the Good Samaritan and the words "Go thou and do likewise." It sounds to me like a recommendation to behave like angels.

GUIDELINES FOR MODELING
OURSELVES
AFTER ANGELS

Healing

• Angels are spirits of action, so always be prepared to offer a helping hand. This might mean spending a few days with your daughter to help her care for a newborn, or with your husband or wife who has just returned from the hospital after major surgery. Or lending someone money to help him get his life together again. Or driving an elderly neighbor to the supermarket.

• Inspire hope. Focus attention on the best of past, present, and future. Help people understand what's going on and what they can do about it, so they can get back in command of their lives. Avoid behavior that makes people feel worse, such as putting them down, criticizing their ideas, finding fault with them, and closing the doors to imagination and unforeseen possibilities that may hold enormous promise.

• Become a confidant to *at least* one person you know. Let those who confide in you know you're there for them, that the door is always open if they wish to turn to you to share happiness or sorrow. Assure them, by your actions and reactions, that they can reveal themselves to you without humiliation and without fear of being controlled or taken advantage of. Assure them, too, that what they tell you will be held in the *strictest confidence*. That's what confidant means.

- Develop a habit of empathy and use it to heal. Understand what others are experiencing in their lives. Listen to them carefully and in a nonjudgmental fashion. Look into yourself to discover how their experiences may correspond to your own past experiences with similar feelings and events.

- Make phone calls or send notes to people you know to be sick, recovering from an illness, or disabled. Dropping by to see them is even better, if it's the appropriate thing to do and if you can. Include people you don't necessarily know that well in your helping and healing efforts.

- Volunteer to make someone happy. A few weeks ago I went to see a patient of mine in a nursing home. The garden was filled with dogs doing an assortment of tricks, one at a time. Twenty or so patients sat around watching with delight. The dogs' owners had taken time away from their other activities to go there and devote a few hours to cheering everyone up. I'm sure you know that animals have a way of doing that.

- If you attend church, join the congregation in their prayers for the sick. If you don't, pray for them anyway.

- Fight stigma. I remember when I was ten years old, my mother had to have a minor operation to remove a tumor of her parotid gland. It's a gland in the mouth that helps digest food, and it appears as a swelling at the base of the jaw. In those days, the stigma surrounding cancer was very real, and, although she didn't have cancer, the doctor who was going to perform the procedure was known as a cancer specialist. So my father arranged for her to be admitted surreptitiously the night before the surgery; she was discharged the next afternoon, and no one was the wiser. Today it's mental illness that is heavily stigmatized, less than it once was, but still quite prevalently. Even something as commonplace as clinical depression, for which we doctors can do a great deal, is considered a weakness or a serious mental aberration by more than 50 percent of Americans. So if you know anyone suffering with a psychiatric problem, give them the same *support and respect* you'd give anyone else, and actively encourage them in their efforts to seek help and to recover.

• If there's anyone you haven't yet forgiven, forgive them now. Let go of old hurts and grievances. You'll not only heal yourself by doing so, but you'll set a wonderful example for others to follow.

XII

THE SEVENTH STRENGTH

Becoming a More Spiritual Person

For those who want a little more out of life (for instance meaning) and those who wouldn't mind living forever

*I*T'S SOMETIMES hard to believe we are spiritual beings. Sitting in front of a computer all day long entering, and retrieving data; watching the evidence of human cruelty on the nightly news; witnessing the small insensitivities and slights that people seem to exchange regularly with each other; being confronted with rudeness, belligerence, selfishness, and greed at every turn; contrasting the opulent mansions of the Hamptons, Nantucket, Beverly Hills, Malibu, and a hundred other places around the world with the dire poverty of city ghettos and the disease-riddled jungles and deserts of underdeveloped nations; being exposed to improprieties, legal wrangling, and lust among politicians; sadly realizing how family life has become so fragmented; watching the steady, ongoing destruction of our natural habitat, the earth; and hearing of the resurgence of the nuclear arms race—how can we really think that human beings are even slightly spiritual? It's even hard sometimes to feel that way in church.

And yet in spite of all the evil around us, most people still do believe in God and in humankind's eternal destiny. That so many people believe doesn't make it true. But the fact that this belief has persisted from the beginning of known time and that it has been embraced by a great many minds a good deal more intelligent than mine is to me sufficient evidence that there must be something to it. Then too you have angel manifestations that cannot be explained without acknowledging that both they and we share a common bond of spirituality.

What does spirit mean? It doesn't mean ghosts. It has nothing to do with seances or wisps of smoke and the clanking of chains in old English houses. And things aren't spiritual just because you can't see or hear them; after all, there were radio waves before we ever knew they existed, and they're certainly not of the spirit.

Another word for spirit is soul, although you don't hear it used as much today as it once was. All living beings were said to have souls. Plants have souls. Animals have souls. We have souls. *The difference between our souls and those that belong to the rest of nature is that one aspect of our soul is spiritual and, presumably, immortal.* I must confess that thinking of owls and chipmunks and rhododendrons and dogwood trees as having souls makes me feel even more appreciative of and respectful toward these other forms of life on earth.

There's something more than our physical being, something that once created goes on forever. It can't be material, because matter doesn't last forever. It must be nonmatter, and nonmatter is spirit, unbound by time and space, only transiently wedded to the flesh, a place of thought and will, an identity. It's my spirit that is truly me and your spirit that is truly you, far more singular and unique than your Social Security number, your fingerprints, your DNA. Our spiritual selves are the true bearers of our individuality.

And the spiritual is what we have most in common with the angels. I sometimes think I see a flash of immortality in the eyes of a three-month-old infant. It is as if, at birth, the child possesses the knowledge and wisdom of angels—maybe that's why we often refer to them as little angels—and that in the course of a lifetime, as brain structures develop, skills are mastered, experiences experienced, the child's awareness of the way things *really* are becomes steadily more and more obscured, as in Wordsworth's *Intimations Ode*: "Our birth is but a sleep and a forgetting."

When my daughter Winnie was three, she sat on the edge of my bed and looked over at my dresser, where a photo of my late mother sat. She pointed at it. "That's your mother," she said.

"Yes," I replied.

"My grandmother," she said.

Again I said yes.

"I knew her," Winnie said, taking me by surprise.

"You couldn't have known her, Winnie. She died before you were born."

She looked thoughtful and then said, "Oh, but I did. She sent me to you."

I asked Winnie when she was thirteen years old, if she remembered that incident. She nodded. "Now that you're grown up," I asked, "what do you think about what you said."

Without hesitation, she replied, "I said it. I meant it." And she wouldn't discuss the matter more.

What might this mean? It could be a child's imagination. Years later, when she confirmed it, she might have been trying to be kind, not wanting to disturb my memory of a pleasant anecdote. Then again, it could have been true. Perhaps there is a place where souls wait to come to earth, join with flesh, become human beings, live out their lives, and return again to life beyond death. So far, nobody can either prove or disprove this possibility.

Here on earth our spirits are inextricably bound together with our bodies and with our psychological selves, our psyches. You can't see the psyche or hold it in your hand either. But what is it? Electrical and chemical impulses traveling through brain circuitry, accounting for consciousness, judgment, action, memory, emotion? The activation of cortical and subcortical regions of the central nervous system associated with the experience of loving? An enjoyment of sound in the form of music that winds its way up the acoustic nerve to the appropriate reception centers from whence it spreads out to affect the regions of joy, sorrow, excitement, or contentment? The shaping of our adult perceptions by life experiences that happened a long time ago when we were children? It is all this, and much more. *The psyche is the place where body and spirit meet and, while we are confined to earth, through which the spirit makes itself known and acts.*

WHAT SPIRITUALITY DOES FOR US

Spirituality gives meaning to our lives. Whether I'm working with patients or talking with friends, the question that inevitably enters my mind is What does this experience mean to them? I often ask myself the same question too. What does graduating from college mean to me? What does getting married, having children, watching and guiding them as they grow up, celebrating a thirtieth birthday or a sixtieth one mean to me? What have these events, and similar milestones, meant to you?

Life is filled with successes and failures. It's the rare person who does not know moments of triumph and hours of defeat. Life has its ups and downs, and the context within which we interpret what is happening plays a critical role in our ability to understand and deal with it. I recall once asking a sixty-eight-year-old patient what the most important turning point in his life was. I already knew him pretty well. I thought he was going to say it was the day his son was born, after he and his wife had tried so hard and for so long to conceive; or maybe the time his patrol was caught in a surprise ambush by North Korean troops, and only he and two others escaped alive.

Instead he said: "You know I had a nervous breakdown when I was in my forties. I went to the hospital. I was terribly depressed. My wife and I were having serious problems, and my business was in deep trouble, and

I just fell apart. One day I thought I was fine. Three weeks later I found myself in the admissions unit of the Psychiatric Institute being examined by a resident who told me I reminded him of a case of battle fatigue. I was placed on a locked unit, because they weren't sure whether I was suicidal. I thought of killing myself, but I didn't intend to, even though I was feeling a terrible ache that seemed to go all through me. A few days after I got there, I decided to use what little energy I could find to take a shower. I stood there, hurting, wanting to die, the water pouring down on me. I felt utterly hopeless. Then, suddenly, I thought of Jesus, dying on the cross, and I thought, Who am I to feel so sorry for myself? I took a couple of deep breaths. Then I looked up at the shower head and let the water spill over my face, and I said to myself, I offer this up, my pain, the embarrassment of being in this place, to my God, in my own small way to share in the suffering of the universe. And I could feel the anguish falling away from me, as if it were being carried off down the drain with the water.

"I've never been the same since. I mean, sure I'm the same person. But that experience put me in more immediate contact with my spirit than I've ever been, before or since. It helped me regain perspective and realize that my faith and hope and ultimate trust in God were my real sources of strength and of knowing who I am."

I hadn't expected this answer to my question at all. But, knowing that my patient had been a fairly religious person most of his life, I shouldn't have been surprised. Then again, just being religious and participating in religious ritual does not at all guarantee that a person is truly in touch with his or her spiritual nature, as my patient surely was.

". . .my real sources of strength and of knowing who I am." It's being aware of your spiritual nature that does that for you. Here is the power that allows you to assume your place in the universe. It gives meaning to life. It offers hope, as, like Tennyson's Ulysses, we journey through "that untravell'd world whose margin fades for ever and for ever when I move." It provides a roadmap for our journey through life. It motivates us to strive to do the right thing. It enriches the quality of our lives as little else can. It is a source of happiness when things go well, and of the courage and endurance we need when they don't. It's a badge of honor. It's what makes us like the angels.

A HABIT OF SPIRITUALITY

If spirituality is a characteristic of a being—angels are wholly spirit and we partly so—why refer to it as one of the seven strengths of successful angels? It's what they are. What one is isn't exactly a habit. Using one's will for willing and one's mind for knowing, communicating, healing, protecting, loving—these are clearly talents that can become habitual. But spirituality? Where does this fit in?

To begin with, spirituality provides us with the energy and direction that empowers us to make a habit of these other gifts and to use them only for ends that are inherently good. Consider how much easier it is to respect and love and give to others when you think that they too are spiritual beings. It is *the* common denominator among all people, regardless of gender, race, creed, or nationality, and hence the most effective way to eliminate prejudice, an evil rooted in accidents of birth. How much easier it is to listen and try to understand someone when you realize that what you are trying to understand is spiritual too. It is easier to reach out to comfort when you know that you are comforting not only the body but the soul as well. It can only make you a better husband or wife, parent or child, doctor or teacher or mutual fund manager or engineer.

There's a scene that I found particularly moving in the film *As Good As It Gets*, starring Jack Nicholson and Helen Hunt. They're sitting in a restaurant, and she has asked Nicholson to say something nice to her. He wrinkles up his face a bit, something he is famous for, looks directly at her, and says quietly, "You make me want to be a better person." I don't analyze movies while I'm watching them. I simply try to live the experience of them. It's only now, months later, that I realize that in this scene, the spirits of these two people reach out to touch each other, only for an instant, of course, because Nicholson quickly puts his foot in his mouth again, and it takes the rest of the story for his better self to emerge.

This scene provides a clue to discovering ways in which we can develop habits that will continually acknowledge and enrich our spirituality. There's not a day that passes when you don't have a chance to help someone else become a better person. And that doesn't mean there has to be something wrong with the other person. I mean, he or she doesn't have to be short-tempered or caustic or bigoted or ungiving. If you can help with these kind of shortcomings, fine. But every one of us can do better, in one way or another, especially with a little help from our friends. We can choose better, learn better, communicate better, love better, pray better. There's always room for improvement.

Nor do I wish to imply that helping someone become more in touch with his or her spirituality has to involve confrontation or critique. In fact, spirituality is usually such a private thing that you often have to be careful about talking of it at all. The most effective way to go about it, it seems to me, is by thought and example. The quiet knowledge of your own spirituality will communicate itself to others wordlessly, intuitively, which some believe to be how angels communicate. People will sense it, even if they cannot quite define it, and hopefully this message will encourage them to be open to their own spirituality.

There'll be something *special* about the way you care, about your optimism when times are tough, about the respect you show to others because they're special too, about your readiness to forgive, about your honesty and forthrightness, about your tolerance and egalitarianism (which means the way you treat everyone more or less the same), about your sense of purpose in life.

Now, this certainly doesn't mean that you tiptoe around in a fog, wearing a perpetual smile, and think of yourself as spiritual all day long. Nobody could function in the world like that. I don't think of myself as spiritual when I'm driving a car in New York City traffic, or lunching with a friend, or shopping for clothes at an outlet mall. And I never try to walk through doors or float across the room. In fact, I don't think about being spiritual most of the time. I do when I pray, I suppose, and when I contemplate life, when I think about who and what I am and where my life is going. But the really nice thing about spirituality is that, once you accept that it is the very real and very comfortable center of your being, you can think about it any time you choose.

It must already be obvious that whenever you walk in the footsteps of angels, you're growing spiritually. And whenever you think about God, and say a prayer of thanks because something nice has happened, or maybe just because it's an especially beautiful day, you enrich your spirit.

Religion is where each person's spiritual life comes together. The word *religion* means a "binding back," more specifically, a binding back to God. It begins in the heart. Faith in God is just that, faith, a belief in what we can neither prove nor disprove, since proof eliminates the need for faith. I must say I sometimes wonder why God chose to make acceptance of his existence a matter of faith. Now that we have all these wonderful means to communicate electronically, why doesn't God just preempt prime time programs on television and make his presence unmistakably clear? Obviously, that's not what he has in mind.

So we're stuck with the need for faith. And although there is much to be said for joining together with other people to express our faith, as in going to weekly services, the faith that counts is the faith that resides within our own spirits. In my initial consultation with patients, I routinely ask them their age, marital status, the names and ages of any children, the kind of work they do, their home and business addresses and telephone numbers, and their religious persuasion, if any.

I recently asked a young woman what her religion was. She replied, "None." So I put "none" on my record. A little later in the interview, she made a passing reference to praying. "When I asked you about religion earlier, you said none," I said. "Where does praying fit in?" "Oh," she replied. "I thought you meant 'religion.' I believe in God. It's a personal thing. I just don't belong to any formal church."

Traditionally, most psychiatrists and many psychotherapists ignore the spiritual and religious lives of their patients. Many years ago a leading psychiatrist, Fritz Redlich, studied the effect that various qualities of the therapist-patient relationship had on the outcome of treatment and concluded that those patients who fared best were under the care of therapists with similar backgrounds and values. If Redlich's observations were correct, and experience tells me they were, how can a therapist who has no faith in God or spirituality successfully treat a patient who does? It's estimated that 80 percent of Americans, but only about 30 percent of psychiatrists, believe in God. I don't know what the figures are for other psychotherapists. But it does sound as though, if you value your spirituality and need to get into therapy, you'd do well to find someone who shares your beliefs, or at least has genuine respect for them.

The obvious advantage in belonging to a spiritual community is the fact that a congregation gives you the opportunity to magnify the power of your prayers. There is strength in numbers. It's also strengthening to be with others who publicly acknowledge their spiritual essence. Then too you can hear readings from the Bible and hopefully hear an inspiring homily. In some faiths, you have Communion as well. Formal religion also tries to provide guidelines that you can follow to lead more spiritual lives. A side benefit of belonging is the sense of belonging itself, and the chance to make friends with people who share your world view and a lot of other things as well, such as playing tennis or bridge, or going to concerts, or having cookouts on Memorial Day and the Fourth of July.

You may even be reminded of angels. I recently went to a christening in a church in Boston. One of the first things I noticed were two gigantic statues of angels standing on either side of the sanctuary. I'd been in the same church once before but had never noticed them. I looked up at the ceiling and saw more angels there, not Michelangelo's angels, of course, but angels carved of wood, gilded, smiling as angels are portrayed as smiling, watching over us below.

GUIDELINES FOR MODELING OURSELVES AFTER ANGELS

Spirituality

- Acknowledge your spiritual self. Value it greatly.

- Acknowledge and respect everyone else's spiritual reality, and let this govern your attitudes and behavior toward all human beings.

- If you believe in God, thank Him every day for your existence and for the wonderful gifts He has given you. Even if you don't, or can't be sure about it, you can lead a very meaningful life by being angel-like without ever having to think about angels, leaving the world a little better a place than it was when you arrived.

- When you feel desperate, call on God for hope and enlightenment. When you're in pain, ask Him for the courage to bear it. When you're afraid, remind yourself of the sparrows and the lilies of the field and His reassurance that He will always look after you.

- Find a book or two with spiritual messages, ones that appeal to you, and read from them a few minutes every day for inspiration and comfort.

- Live your spiritual life quietly and with modesty. Let others discern it in your spiritually guided behavior, your caring for others, your values, your commitment to good.

- Don't be dissuaded from your faith by the evils in this world. These are often cited as a reason for not believing. In fact, they give us all an opportunity to exercise virtue. In the face of cruelty, you can be kind. In the face of injustice, you can be firm and unyielding. In the face of hatred, you can be loving. There's so much wrong in this world that I simply can't believe it's all our fault. I have to think that something else is afoot, such as the power of fallen angels. In the face of devils, you can become more like the angels of God.

- Avoid cults and strange beliefs that stand in defiance of God, including those that may sound innocent enough, but which, rather than honoring God, worship mankind instead.

- Be tolerant and understanding toward those whose religious practices differ from yours. Each person must serve God as he or she believes proper.

- Maximize your spirituality by joining together with others who are committed to the same end. In this way you can greatly strengthen your own faith while helping them to strengthen theirs.

Forever honored be the Tree
Whose Apple Winterworn
Enticed to Breakfast from the Sky
Two Gabriels Yestermorn.

They registered in Nature's Book
As Robins—Sire and Son —
But Angels have that modest way
To screen them from Renown.

Poem Number 1570
EMILY DICKINSON

Angel
Strategies

XIII

Angel Strategies

In which you will learn how to prevail over ordinary and extraordinary temptations and human frailties and to avoid the fate of fallen angels

THE MOST powerful enemies of our happiness, fulfillment, and spirituality are the seven deadly sins: Pride, Envy, Greed, Lust, Sloth, Gluttony, and . . .I frequently have trouble recalling the seventh. It's Anger. I'm sure that's because anger can be both healthy and unhealthy, good and bad, a problem when it's expressed violently or in the wrong place at the wrong time toward the wrong issue or the wrong person, and a problem when it goes unrecognized, unfelt, unexpressed at all.

Hate's a better word for the seventh sin.

From the beginning of time, these sins have done people in. We know the harm they've produced, from embezzlement to murder. Fortunately, few, if any of us have all seven vulnerabilities, or even a majority of them. More often we are subject to one or two particular faults that we must guard against by emulating the good sense, love, and spirituality of angels.

I'M THE MOST IMPORTANT PERSON AROUND

Too much pride is what did Lucifer and his followers in, so it's certainly something we'd better guard against, lest we suffer a similar awful fate.

"Most of the harm that's done in the world is done by people trying to think well of themselves," says Sir Henry Harcourt Reilly in T. S. Eliot's play *The Cocktail Party* . On the surface, that observation seems to run counter to what we believe in. Wander down the mile-long self-help aisles of you local bookstore and you'll find volume after volume offering ways for you to think better of yourself. It's been my job, as a doctor, to help people give up negative self-images ("I'm a worthless, inadequate failure as a person") in favor of more positive ones ("I'm all right, even if I haven't done everything the way I should and could have"). My efforts often center on helping people make the important distinction between their failures and accomplishments, thoughts and feelings, strengths and limitations and *who they really are*.

Psychiatrists have a term to describe self-love: narcissism. They even have a diagnostic category for people who are concerned only with their own needs and whose relationships with others are dominated by their own selfishness: narcissistic personality disorder. The word *narcissism* derives from the mythological story of Narcissus, who so admired his own image reflected in a pool of water that he fell into the pool and drowned. Theoretically, every infant is narcissistic. Healthy development requires the gradual recognition that one is not the center of the universe, nor the only creature in it. This may come as a shock. But the trauma is ameliorated by realizing that relating to others can be good, comforting, rewarding, reassuring, helpful; and eventually that, giving love is as wonderful as receiving it; and that one's own significance, especially since it is a spiritual significance, need not be compromised in the process.

But a lot of damage can happen during this process. Should you have a mother who is depressed or just isn't there for you or doesn't love you or frankly rejects you, it's not so easy to make the leap toward accepting your place in a world of others. Or you may be utterly spoiled, like George Miniver Amberson in Booth Tarkington's classic novel (and Orson Welles' brilliant film) *The Magnificent Ambersons*, whose selfishness makes a major contribution toward his family's unhappiness and decline. Or maybe you simply never got the message and have spent your life in the pursuit of power, wealth, sexual conquest, and whatever else seemed to do the trick of making you feel like the most important person alive. Consider the final scene of the film *White Heat*. James Cagney, pursued by police, is standing on top of a huge gas storage tank. Seconds before he fires his gun into it, his pride wells up and he shouts at the top of his lungs, "Made it, ma. Top of the world, ma!" And he disappears in the massive explosion that follows.

ANGEL STRATEGIES: HUMILITY

Who you are is always something special. What makes you special isn't how much money you have, what kind of work you do, how big your house is, or how much education you've got under your belt—not that I'll deny that some of these things do and should make us feel pretty good about ourselves. But our true significance comes from being human beings, a very important part of which is spiritual. What could be more uplifting?

What could be more humbling? Every gardener knows the origin of the word *humble*. It comes from *humus*, the soil you put on things that grow to help them grow. Too often, we mistakenly picture the humble person as one who grovels before the powerful, lacking in self-confidence, pathetically unassertive, and without a trace of reasonable pride. Yet *human* and *humility* share the same origin: created from the earth.

I shall always remember a scene from a Spanish black-and-white film production of *Don Quixote*. A column of princes and bishops ride tall on their magnificent horses, while ahead of them several robed monks walk, swinging incense and chanting, "Dust we are, to dust we shall return."

One of the most salient comments regarding humility that I have read is found in Thomas Merton's *Seeds of Contemplation*. Merton writes:

> In humility is the greatest freedom. As long as you have to defend the imaginary self that you think is important, you lose your peace of heart. As soon as you compare that shadow with the shadows of other people, you lose all joy, because you have begun to trade in unrealities, and there is no joy in things that do not exist.

As soon as you begin to take yourself seriously and imagine that your virtues are important because they are yours, you become the prisoner of your own vanity and even your best works will blind and deceive you. Then, in order to defend yourself, you will begin to see sins and faults everywhere in the actions of other men. And the more unreasonable importance you attach to yourself and to your own works, the more you will tend to build up your own idea of yourself by condemning other people. Some of the most virtuous men in the world are also the bitterest and most unhappy, because they have unconsciously come to believe that all their happiness depends on their being more virtuous than other men.

When humility delivers a man from attachment to his own works and his own reputation, he discovers that true joy is only possible when we have completely forgotten ourselves. And it is only when we pay no more attention to our own life and our own reputation and own excellence that we are at last completely free to serve God.

ALL I WANT IS EVERYTHING, AND EVEN THAT'S NOT ENOUGH

"I have plenty of money, my own jet airplane—well, it belongs to the company, but in effect it's mine—three homes, a BMW, the big one, and I've been a guest at the White House six times."

The person saying this to me was the CEO of one of the *Fortune* 500 companies. He did not seem to be the least bit troubled by the avarice and love of power that his remarks revealed. I asked him if he were happy. "Sure," he replied. "Who wouldn't be?"

I asked him what it had cost him to get where he was.

"I've been divorced twice, but then everyone gets divorced these days. I only have kids by my second marriage. Their mother has done her best to keep me from seeing them, but I learned to live without them. No great loss. I don't have that much free time anyway." He paused. "My oldest son died of an overdose, but that was his own doing," he said, lowering his voice slightly. "I'm a little resentful I didn't make the *Forbes* 400 rich list. My health's not the best, I have high blood pressure and have had one coronary bypass, but I can afford the best doctors anyone can buy. I suppose I'm afraid of getting old. And, yes, my present wife is pretty close to being an alcoholic."

"Was it worth it?" I then asked.

"Absolutely," he answered without hesitation.

Greed is a miserable business. *Miser* and *misery* have the same word origin. You may be able to ignore the misery as you sit on the porch of your multimillion-dollar oceanfront home and your butler serves drinks to the half-dozen celebrities you've invited for the weekend. While it's safe to say that greed can play an important part in the accumulation of wealth, the mere fact that you may be wealthy does not necessarily mean you're greedy. I know very well-to-do people who have never lost touch with their spirituality. But they are a decided minority. . . consider how painful it must be to be greedy if you haven't the dubious compensation of having amassed a storehouse of material things, for instance Picasso paintings, diamond pendants, or memorabilia that once belonged to John F. Kennedy. Imagine the pain of desperately wanting things and never being able to have them. Small greed, big greed—it's all the same.

It all involves an enormous appetite for material things, an insatiable craving that stems from selfishness, from a need for extraordinary power, at times from a deeply hidden unhappiness. Greed makes it very difficult for the greedy individual to attend to many other important aspects of the human experience, such as love, justice (the acquisition of wealth often, though not always, requires a disregard for the rights, privileges, and well-being of others), and affairs of the spirit. So inevitably family, friends, and colleagues become its victims. It creates a passionate attachment to the things one has accumulated, an addiction to money and what money buys, and a consequent fear of losing any part of what one has. Even the appearance of generosity may not entirely conceal the greed that made the generosity possible; it may reflect a genuine change of heart, a wish to give on a large scale what one failed to give in a more personal way over the years; or it may be another form of greed, the desire for fame and immortality in someone who has failed to appreciate the immortality of the spirit.

ANGEL STRATEGIES: GENEROSITY

When angels aren't shedding tears because the people they've been assigned to guide and protect are awash in greed, they're probably laughing at the futility of such ambitions. "Vanity of vanities and all is vanity. . .This is the greatest wisdom—to seek the kingdom of heaven through contempt of the world. It is vanity, therefore, to see and trust in riches that perish" wrote St. Thomas a Kempis. Angels know these lines by heart. They may even have inspired them.

"Contempt" is a pretty strong word. I can't believe that it was intended to make us truly disdain the wonderful gifts on earth that have been provided for us. A gentler synonym is "disregard," implying that we are best served by an enjoyment of them without making them the be-all and end-all of our lives. In a proper hierarchy of values, our spirituality should come first, but there's nothing wrong with wanting enough money to live in a nice house, send your children to the best colleges they can get into, entertain friends, own a safe automobile, travel, invest wisely, and save for your retirement. Material comfort is a well-deserved reward for hard work. Occasionally you may even get rich in the process. It's not so much the amount of money you make but how you make it and regard it that matters.

I know a young man who majored in economics and headed for Wall Street to become an apprentice in investment banking. He worked twelve-hour days and often on weekends, and he observed that even the senior members of the firm were equally immersed in their work. He didn't consider this out of line. His friends who had gone into medicine were working just as hard. But he grew troubled by what his work involved. The rewards eventually could be spectacular, true enough. And he liked the idea of becoming wealthy. But he also wondered whether he wanted to devote his life to raising billions of dollars so that AT&T or IBM or Exxon could acquire other companies or build new plants or drill for more oil. Someone had to do this, he realized, although he considered that his colleagues' goals had more to do with the money they were making than the good their clients might accomplish with it. In fact, they seemed singularly indifferent to such matters. After three years on the Street, he quit to go into business for himself, joining with a couple of friends to develop an information service for the Internet. Within six years he was worth more than two million dollars. "Maybe it's not as much as I would have made had I stayed with investment banking, but it's enough for me. I work just as hard, but I'm my own boss. I just got married, and my work style gives me the time to spend with my wife and to have a family. And I feel that what we're doing is really worthwhile, putting all kinds of valuable data at the fingertips of anyone who can learn to use a computer."

Getting your priorities in order is one way for you to protect yourself from the ravages of greed. Another is to practice generosity, of time and attention as well as money. Material miserliness isn't hard to spot; it can be corrected by making the effort to part with money with more grace and to share what you have with others more freely and in a cheerful way. But emotional miserliness is often more subtle. The same people who hoard their money tend to hoard their feelings too. "I don't like to tell my husband that I love him," one woman patient told me. "It makes me feel uncomfortable. In fact, it's as if something's being taken away from me to say it." I encouraged her to make the effort, pointing out that it would involve more generosity—a quality she admired in the abstract—on her part to do this than for someone to whom these words came easily. She made the effort and eventually was able to say "I love you" much more naturally, and she felt better for having done so.

The antidotes to greed are love and spirituality. Because greed is essentially materialistic, it's hard to envision a greedy angel. I can consider a proud one or an envious one but not a greedy one. By the same token, we can reduce our risk of falling prey to greed by cultivating the strengths of angels.

I WANT WHAT YOU HAVE, EVEN IF I HAVE TO KILL YOU TO GET IT

Envy is another deadly sin we share with angels. Instead of being ecstatic about the wonderful existence they enjoyed thanks to God, a number of angels envied God, and, it is said, envied human beings too. They rebelled and were thrown out of heaven into hell, or hell on earth. You could say they lost perspective. Their attention was caught by what they didn't have rather than by what they did. Does that sound familiar? The angels we've set out to emulate are those who kept their perspective, happy to be who and what they were, angels, and all that went along with being angels.

As it happens, envy's not my particular weakness. I can count on the fingers of one hand, the number of times that I've felt even a twinge of envy. Maybe being a physician and knowing what *really* goes on in the lives of other people taught me early on that I'd rather not trade places with anybody. You know, you can't just pick and choose the one thing you wish you had. Life doesn't work that way. You have to take the whole package, the best and the worst of it. I think if you take the time to learn all the facts about the lives of people you have envied, you'd probably prefer to be yourself too.

But I've encountered plenty of envy and watched it take malicious forms. I've seen talented employees thwarted in their progress in a company or an academic setting because of envious superiors. I've seen women hate their husbands, fathers hate their sons, friends denigrate friends, all because of envy: Good looks, quick mind, physical strength, professional success, youth. And I know there's neither profit nor joy in it for either the envier or the object of his or her envy.

Jealousy is not the same as envy, but it can be just as destructive. Whereas envy involves wanting what someone else has and hating him or her for having it, jealousy has to do with love, or at least a strong attachment for another human being. A jealous lover is someone who suspects that the person he or she loves has been unfaithful and is involved with someone else. Sexual passion is often a part of it. Such jealousy may be the product of one's insecurity or possessiveness, or it may be valid. Another common setting for jealousy is in relationships between family members or friends. Correctly or or not, you may feel that your parents love your brother or sister more than they love you, or that your friend Doris cares more for another friend, Alice, than she does for you. In either case, if your jealousy and the hatred it generates get out of hand, it can lead to dire, and even deadly, consequences.

ANGEL STRATEGIES: CONTENTMENT

Angels are happy being angels. We should be happy being ourselves, which is not to say that there isn't always room for improvement. If you carefully assess yourself—who you are, what you have, what you honestly desire, how you might best use your talents and take advantage of opportunities (and challenges) as they present themselves—and use this self-assessment as your point of reference for your level of contentment in the present and your ambition for the future, you won't need to envy anyone else.

Charlie was the son of friends of mine, who was painfully envious of his younger brother Ed. Ed had been an honor student in high school and was then in his third year at Yale University, where he was also excelling in his studies. He intended to enter law school after graduation.

Charlie, on the other hand, had attended a small, not very well-known college, where his performance had been quite mediocre. After graduation, he had no idea what career path to follow, so he took the first job he was offered, as a telemarketer with a personal computer company. He did his work adequately but without much enthusiasm.

Any mention of Ed and how well Ed was doing made Charlie boil inside. When the family got together for Christmas Eve that year, he could hardly conceal his resentment, and he made it generally unpleasant for everyone there.

Ed could have reacted with anger. He didn't. Instead, he responded to it with angel-like generosity, making quiet and carefully timed references to Charlie's strong points—he was handsome, related easily to people, was already making a pretty good living, and was lucky enough to have an attractive, loving girlfriend of whom everyone in the family was very fond. Ed didn't miss an opportunity to compliment Charlie, and to do so in such a way that Charlie never detected his purpose.

And Ed was quite frank and open about his own life. Sure, he said, his career was going along great. But he'd just broken up with a girl he'd been very much in love with, and he was upset about that. He was concerned about how much he owed in student loans and how he'd be able to pay them back. "Nobody has it all," he said. "But I'm happy. Even when I'm worried, I'm happy."

He could see Charlie's mind working overtime. By the time midnight arrived and everyone wished each other a Merry Christmas, the grim look on his face had been replaced by a pleasant smile. In the months that followed, Ed and Charlie grew to become real friends.

Whether you have to contend with envy or jealousy, developing angel strengths is the way to go. Use your will to dismiss destructive thoughts that arise from these passions. Use your knowledge to gain perspective, appreciating that every human being has his or her private pain. Use your generosity to wish others well rather than wanting to take something away from them.

Don't set yourself up to be a target of envy. Avoid ostentatiousness. Be modest about your achievements. Don't give anyone with whom you're emotionally involved grounds to be jealous. If you're not contented in the relationship, change it or end it. If you happen to be the object of unwarranted jealousy, put the other person's uncertainty to rest as best you can. Don't take offense. And don't make things worse by playing coy.

Fear and hate can be dangerous allies.

I HATE. . . [FILL IN THE BLANK]

I recently met with the members of an editorial board of a journal of which I am editor. We were exploring topics for the upcoming issues. Most of these were clinical and scientific. However, one of my colleagues remarked that he had never before observed so much hatred in people. "Hate?" I asked to be sure I had heard him correctly. He nodded. Others began to speak up in agreement. Not just anger, but seething rage. "We have an epidemic in the making," one doctor said grimly.

The nightly news reports confirm the presence of powerful, destructive forces at work in the world. It seems almost ironic, considering the fact that human beings have never before enjoyed such material comfort and security against a host of once commonplace diseases and environmental dangers. Even those who still live in poverty and want, who still search for human freedom and dignity, can have more hope than ever before that the political and scientific advances of the more developed nations will spill over into theirs, and perhaps in the not-too-distant future.

Some of the hatred we see is born out of envy, some out of injustice, some out of fear of an unpredictable future resulting from dramatic technologic change and of the consequences of sins committed against earth itself. Greed and selfishness are even threatening the existence of frogs, which, as you may know, are considered by the Chinese to be a sign of good fortune and have long been the delight of children of all ages, myself included—witness Mr. Toad of Toad Hall in Kenneth Grahame's *The Wind in the Willows*, and television's Kermit the Frog.

It is a hatred that is born out of prejudice and paranoia, helplessness, a painful sense of personal insignificance, and a profound discontent resulting from being out of touch with the spirit within us. The events of the twentieth century are filled with evidence of this hatred—war, the slaughter of innocent children, attempts to eradicate entire populations. Its prevalence today may be one reason why more and more people are looking to angels to protect us in this hour of our need.

Now, there's another kind of anger with which we're more personally familiar: feeling mad and losing your temper; and why not, if you or someone close to you has been on the receiving end of an insult or injustice? There are times when only expressing your outrage will get the results you're after. There are even times when only a show of annoyance will get your children to wash behind their ears and get ready for bed.

This is healthy anger.

It's unhealthy and unwise to overreact, becoming furious at a relatively minor slight, for example, or allowing anger to become the start of enduring resentment. But not recognizing and coming to terms with anger when it's there, or should be there, can also be decidedly unhealthy. Many people are so afraid of being angry, so emotionally suffocated, that they don't even feel anger. The emotion will express itself, of course, in

other ways, such as physical maladies, mental immobi-
lization, or behavior patterns that secretly get the message across, for instance, being habitually late for work
or repeatedly saying things that provoke someone else
to be mad instead.

ANGEL STRATEGIES: LOVE, UNDERSTANDING, AND FORGIVENESS

I don't know whether angels get angry. I have no way of
knowing whether they were angry when they fought
the devil and his legions or when they drove Adam and
Eve out of the Garden of Eden or when they wiped out
the Assyrians in the time of Hezekiah, or whether they
were simply going about their business as they'd been
asked to do. Angels, can be militant at times. But
there's no place in their souls for hate. Maybe they get
a bit impatient with us for our failings, but they certainly don't carry a grudge. Even if they have never felt
anger as we feel anger, they're surely smart enough to
know what human anger is, and to encourage us to find
out what the *real* causes of our angry moods may be and
resolve them.

I have a friend who used to get so mad he'd pound
the walls with his fists and scream obscenities at his
wife. He didn't like being that way. But he didn't seem
able to do anything about it. I thought he might be
depressed underneath his anger and told him so, but he
reacted only by getting angry at me. When he went for
his annual physical examination, his doctor started him
on one of the new antidepressant drugs. Lo and behold,
within a month his outbursts had vanished altogether.

The treatment worked because his depression had a physical component to it which the medication served to alleviate.

I've already mentioned that angels must understand the power of forgiveness. It's the only way I know of to avoid or get rid of resentment, the persistence of anger turned into hate, that ends up destroying the one who hates, and not infrequently a lot of other people too. I'm sure you and I have had our share of slights and rejections. We've been the object of unpleasant, even nasty, criticisms; a target of envy; passed over for promotion; uninvited to the party; or just a victim of the fact that nobody likes everybody all the time. The angel in us tells us to make a habit of forgiving, and a habit of meeting hostility with firmness, strength, and love.

Turning the other cheek doesn't mean standing still and taking a beating, and not trying to defend yourself. It sometimes means walking away from meanness; at other times, it calls for confronting meanness with generosity and consideration until it hopefully dies away. A friend of mine told me that his otherwise lovely wife had a bad habit of too often saying hurtful and cutting things to him. For a long time he met her head on, trying to think of equally nasty things to say to her, a stance that was not natural to him, so he never was very good at it.

Then he decided to change his tactics. Depending on what her particular venom of the day happened to be, he would say, "I'm sorry you feel that way," or "That isn't true, but if that's what you believe, I guess I can't do much to change your mind." Sometimes he'd shrug his shoulders and walk away until her angry mood passed on its own. But always he'd try to *understand* what her anger was really all about—whether he had indeed said or done something to distress her, whether she might be upset by some other matter that had nothing to do with him, or whether it was just a mood. And he did not allow himself to become resentful. Over time, her behavior improved substantially. Keep in mind, however, that in most other ways his wife was a lovely and good-hearted person, deserving of his love and well worth the extra thought and work he had *chosen* to put into finding a better way to handle these painful moments.

I'M TOO TIRED FROM WATCHING TELEVISION TO DO ANYTHING NOW

The couch potato is the contemporary example of sloth, mesmerized by the accumulation of tiny dots that compose the picture on the television screen, practically indifferent to what program happens to be on, surfing aimlessly from one channel to the next, leaving tasks and errands undone, declining opportunities for conversation, feeling sometimes too heavy to lift his or her body off the lounge chair even to stretch.

Can you imagine angels glued to television? Maybe they'd enjoy a segment or two of *Touched by an Angel*, or a concert at Carnegie Hall, or the U.S. Open tennis finals, or an old movie on AMC. But they really don't need a TV. They have much better channels of communication.

Angels aren't lazy. They are active and efficient. They get the job done. Consider how effectively the angel Gabriel delivered his message to Mary about the special role she was to play in history. It took him all of thirty seconds to say what he had to say. Cautioning her not to be afraid, he identified where he came from and why he was there—clear, to the point, no nonsense.

In the well-known story of the chapel of the Sisters of Loretto in Santa Fe, New Mexico, in the mid-nineteenth century the original builders forgot to install a staircase to permit access from the chapel floor to the choir loft. Building this after the fact appeared to be an engineering impossibility. The sisters waited, and prayed. One day a stranger arrived, carrying a tool chest containing only a hammer, a saw, and a T-square. He offered to build the staircase for them. No one seems to know how long it took—perhaps six months—and when he was done, the stranger disappeared without asking to be paid for his work. This staircase stands today. Numerous architects who have examined it agree that its design defies explanation. The belief is that the stranger may have been an angel in disguise. He was certainly no slouch.

ANGEL STRATEGIES: GET UP, GET GOING, GET IT DONE

Angel behavior means getting things done in a timely fashion, not letting work pile up to such a point that you're overwhelmed by it. Can you imagine the angel whose job it was to rescue St. Peter from prison saying: "He can wait one more day. I'm too busy singing in the choir, and when I'm finished I know I'll be too tired."

If you want to fight inertia and procrastination, start by setting priorities. What has to been done now? What can wait until later? If you have a leaky pipe threatening to flood your basement, you may have to postpone your shopping trip to wait until the plumber comes to fix it. If you have a report that must be submitted by the end of the week, you may have to put off getting together with friends for an evening on the town.

Become familiar with the resources available to you for the job you have to do. Know what deadlines are in place. Every morning, make notes of the important things you have to do that day. Keep on top of your finances. *That all sounds great, you say, but I don't have the energy or the will. I can't get started. I feel so disorganized. My apartment is cluttered with paper. It's been that way for months. You say I should walk instead of taking taxis, that I should exercise? That's a laugh. I need all the rest I can get. Being on time? I try. But you can't expect me to behave like an angel. They're pure spirit. They don't have this body to drag around after them.*

Stop a minute. Look around you. Do you exist in a world that's without stimulation, except, of course, for your television set? What kind of music do you listen to? What kind of books do you read? What kind of conversations do you have? Do you play any sports? Have you no hobbies? How about plain old goals?

It's no accident that the most motivated students in school and workers on the job have been spurred on to achieve by diligent parents who themselves set an example of energy and purpose and encouraged their children to do likewise. Even when that isn't the case, very successful people I have known have found it within themselves to supply their own ambitions and dreams. One friend of mine grew up in very modest circumstances. His parents were perpetually inattentive. He had to make his own way in life. He loved going to the movies (when films were more story-driven than sensational) and to the library, where he read voraciously, and to a nearby department store, where he could go to the music department and take an album of Beethoven or Ravel into a booth and listen to it all afternoon and no salesperson would bother him. So you *can* do it, on your own, even if there isn't anyone around to push you to be more angel-like in your determination to make something of yourself.

Of course, it's harder that way. I was very fortunate. My mother used to listen to my Latin homework—not that she understood a word of Latin—and my dad would send the better pieces I'd written to his friends in the literary world, and they'd drop me a note of praise, which would, of course, motivate me to write more.

I recall teaching one of my own children how to study. At the time, he was in his first year of high school. He felt overwhelmed by the amount of material he was required to read and then recall for examinations. Consequently, he did less and less work and got poorer and poorer grades. I decided to sit down with him and show him a simple technique I had used myself to make my studying easier. It consisted of highlighting the key points in the text with a yellow marker, so that when the time came to review them they would stand out, and he could absorb them in a fraction of the time he'd previously spent struggling through the entire book. He came away with an average grade of B+ and a whole new sense of confidence in himself.

I remember giving another one of my children a lesson in competence and self-determination. She was three years old. We were sitting at the breakfast table. In front of her was an untouched bowl of cereal.

"I can't eat this," she said plaintively.

"Don't say you can't eat that," I said. "You can eat it if you want to. Just say I won't eat the cereal."

She smiled. "I won't eat the cereal," she said.

"Fine. That's better," I said. "Now eat it." And she happily did.

I wanted it to be a choice. It was a long time ago, and she has made many intelligent choices since then, growing up to be a wonderfully sensitive and self-reliant young woman.

I EAT, THEREFORE I AM

Obesity is a major health problem in this country, and in most instances it's simply the result of eating too much. Of course, sometimes it's genetic; your genes may have set you up to have a lot of fat distributed throughout your body and only the most heroic of efforts can make even a dent in it. Some people gain weight because their metabolism is slow, as when they don't produce enough thyroid hormone, a common and frequently missed condition, especially among adolescent girls and in the elderly.

But the real reasons why so many people are on their way to resembling Friar Tuck or Santa Claus or the fat lady who has to sing before the game is over are no mystery. You're driving along Interstate 95 on your way from Boston to New York. It's time for lunch. You don't want to get off the highway, so you stop for a fast food meal at McDonald's, a burger with cheese, fries, and a milkshake. By the time you reach home, you're exhausted. So instead of fixing a dinner of chicken and vegetables or something else nutritious, you spend the evening munching away on potato chips, a couple of pickles, and a hard-boiled egg you found in the fridge, topped off with some vanilla ice cream filled with Milky Way candy chunks.

You wake up several times during the night as you do many nights. Like Dagwood Bumstead of comic strip fame, you make a raid on the kitchen at least once, to slap a couple of pieces of boiled ham and a slice of Swiss cheese on a roll and add a little mustard. You skip breakfast in the morning, feeling somewhat heroic. Around ten o'clock, the coffee cart comes around and, starved, you finish off a couple of donuts, plain without sugar, of course. Time for a tuna fish sandwich at lunch. Fish is good for you, and it tastes better doused in mayonnaise. You have a few cashews from the can you keep in your desk around three o'clock, just a little treat. Then you head home for dinner, where you have beef stew with potatoes and broccoli (now that's good for you!), and a very tiny piece of chocolate cake for dessert. Oh, and a few saltines with brie at bedtime is the perfect way to finish off the day.

Are you a glutton now? Maybe not. But you might be on your way. If you think the word "glutton" is unattractive, don't look up the synonyms for it in your thesaurus. You'll really get upset. But you don't have to put on a toga and lie on soft cushions, as the Romans did, while servants rush about serving tons of pheasant and wine and rich sherbets, to qualify as a prisoner of your eating habits. Of course, you may not direct all of your attention to eating. You may not even think about it much of the time. It's just something that happens while you're busy doing other things.

ANGEL STRATEGIES: WILL, KNOWLEDGE, DISCIPLINE, AND SUPPORT

Angels don't eat too much and put on weight. In fact, they don't eat at all, and they don't weigh anything either. How can they possibly know what it's like to crave that hot fudge sundae with whipped cream on top?

They do know. It's in their nature to know, and to have compassion, and to help those whose problem is eating too much. They also have provided us with examples of their unique strengths with which, by now, we should be quite familiar, and which we can employ in our efforts.

The first step is to determine whether you do have trouble regulating your food intake and to what degree, and whether this has resulted in your being malnourished or overweight and to what extent. The next is to see if your can identify any special reasons why you eat so much. Maybe you love food. Or maybe you use it as a substitute for something else, such as love, or because you're unhappy or nervous, or just because it's a habit you've had for years and haven't been able or willing to break.

Now comes a combination of angel-like discipline and creativity. Somehow or other, you have to cut down on the calories. Undoubtedly you've tried to lose weight more than once in the past. You may even have succeeded for a while, but eventually your old habit caught up with you. Now, to increase your chances of success, you have to invent new and more effective strategies. You might start by asking a different question. I mean, instead of assuming that will power is your only recourse, you might ask how you'd like to spend the extra time that not eating between meals might give you. If unhappiness is a factor, make out a list of things you think might make you happy and devise a plan to bring some of them about. If anxiety and nervousness contribute, ask yourself how you can be more courageous and what you might do to achieve greater peace of mind, and find it. If you've been stuck on certain foods that aren't good for you, find new ones that are and learn to enjoy them. Even broccoli.

Find a good support group, one that suits your temperament, and stay with it. The central belief of practically every support group is the existence of a power greater than ourselves to whom we can turn to ask assistance in our efforts to change. It may be that your own angel will be the one to carry your message aloft, returning again to you with the strength you need, faster than the blink of an eye.

And then there's lust

The word lust doesn't specifically apply to sexual passion, although that's the way we usually use it. It actually means to "hunger after," "yearn for," or "need;" but it carries with it carnal connotations, which tend to limit its meaning to desires of the flesh. No matter. It's sexual lust we're concerned with here, the lecherous, lascivious desire for sexual experience. Lust is not the sensual passion that can be part of a loving sexual experience. It differs from healthy sexual desire and experience by its wantonness, license, and brutality. It involves using another human being as a thing, primarily for the selfish purpose of one's own physical pleasure. Lust is, by its very nature, dehumanizing. And it accounts in large measure for the spread of sexually transmitted diseases and the high incidence of rape and unwanted pregnancies. It has also played a role in the decline and fall of many once powerful figures in business and government throughout history, and it was the reason the angels were commanded to destroy Sodom and Gomorrah.

ANGEL STRATEGIES: CHOOSE WELL, AND ENJOY SEX IN THE CONTEXT OF LOVE AND COMMITMENT

Sexual desire is one of the most powerful of human instincts. This should come as no surprise, since sex is our way to procreate. Without it the human race might have died out centuries ago. It's also an act of completion in the relationship between two human beings who love and are committed to each other. Sex is certainly physically pleasurable. It's also psychologically fulfilling, an opportunity to give and receive physical excitement, tenderness, intimacy, love, reassurance, and comfort. In its most splendid moments, it is a spiritual experience as well, since it involves respect and caring for one another that unites the very essences of each person.

The first step in avoiding lust is to make a habit of using your free will to choose good over evil, a choice you may have to make many times when it comes to sexuality.

Then you may move on to other choices. Choose the person with whom you hope to share your body and your soul with care. Get to *know* and appreciate each other, because what you are going to do is the most intimate connection two people can make with each other.

From your knowing, love can grow. From your love, a new level of generosity can be discovered. From your togetherness, a new understanding of your spirituality can be achieved.

"What do you like doing best in the world, Pooh?"
"Well," said Pooh, "what I like best–" and then he
had to stop and think. Because although Eating
Honey was a very good thing to do, there was a
moment just before you began to eat it which was
better than when you were, but he didn't know
what it was called. And then he thought that being
with Christopher Robin was a very good thing to
do, and having Piglet near was a very friendly thing
to have; and so, when he had thought it all out, he
said, "What I like best in the whole world is Me and
Piglet going to see You, and You saying 'What about
a little something?' and Me saying, 'Well, I should-
n't mind a little something, should you, Piglet,' and
it being a hummy sort of day outside, and birds
singing."

The House At Pooh Corner
A. A. MILNE

XIV

Being Human's Not All That Bad

In which you'll be reminded how great it can be to be a human being

BY NOW you may be enthusiastic about the prospect of being more like the angels: Using your will to make better choices. Expanding your knowledge and cultivating wisdom. Possessing more effective communication skills. Exercising greater leadership. Being filled with selfless love and generosity. Being immensely strong, yet humble. Becoming incredibly effective in your new life.

It sounds too good to be true. It *is* too good to be true, because we're not angels and we will never be. We cannot, in this world, come close to their level of perfection. We are human beings, mixtures of clay and spirit. But that isn't the worst thing in the world to be. After all, you could have been one of the fallen angels, whom forgiveness will forever elude.

There's a lot to be said for being human, which is what we were intended to be. We've been given wonderful gifts and opportunities for experiences that even angels cannot share. Feelings, for example. I don't wish to imply that angels do not have emotions, but they can't *experience* emotions as we do. You need a body to experience physical love, for example. Angel love is inherently selfless. Angels are the ultimate altruists. But their love appears to be a function of their will. They will the good of others, but this is quite different from the feelings of love that humans know. No passion there. No infatuation. No romance. No sexuality. These kinds of love have been gifted to us, along with the joy that accompanies such loving. Only people can experience the happiness of becoming parents, the excitement of holding a new infant, the sense of accomplishment and fulfillment to be found in friendship with children who have grown to adulthood and lead their own lives but are still engaged in a relationship of love and loyalty to their parents. Only human beings can experience love that begins as an attraction to someone seen from a distance and progresses through an introduction to a date, to a getting to know one another, to falling in love and intellectually confirming the integrity of such love, to a commitment and a sharing of life's experience together.

We're also the only ones who experience the emotional pain that can be a part of loving, the pain of loss and of loneliness. Angels don't feel physical pain either. Now, only a fool would intentionally seek out pain. There's nothing pleasant about it. I've seen enough patients in emotional and physical pain to realize that. But pain does offer us the opportunity to be courageous.

It provides us with insight into other people's pain. It can, as in the case of the pain of being depressed, be the start of a new level of spirituality if we know enough to use it for such a purpose.

Angels don't cry. Nowhere in the Hebrew Scriptures or the New Testament is there an instance of an angel shedding tears. Jesus cried, but he was part human. We cry. We cry when we're in pain and when we're sad. We cry when we are moved by a beautiful story or an especially gorgeous sunset. Angels may be the most gifted of musicians, so it is believed, but only human beings can be moved to tears by a symphony or a ballad that touches our hearts.

They can't hold hands in the movies. They can't enjoy a delicious meal, a hot cup of chocolate after a cold day out in the snow, the wonderment of diving deep below the surface of the sea and playing with the dolphins, the excitement of putting paint to canvas, the thrill of cheering our home school football team on to victory, or the contentment of having a "little something" on a "hummy sort of day."

Even as we work to develop angel-like behavior, we should rejoice in the fact that we are human, in spite of our frailties and the risk of falling prey to the lure of evil. People don't think about sin much these days, because we don't quite understand what it is and how the concept of sin applies to us. But, as psychiatrist Karl Menninger wrote in his book *The Vital Balance*, the "deemphasis on sin is as unrealistic as the pessimistic conclusion that man is all evil." If you look up the meaning of the word *sin*, you'll be able to separate it from your image of the wild-eyed preacher threatening us with hell and damnation and begin to grasp its real significance. Sin means "to transgress," "to do wrong." Nothing very complicated about that. It also means "to offend." You can do wrong against yourself (choosing evil over good, or just failing to become the person you have the potential to be), against other people (hurting them, treating them with disrespect), and against the earth itself (making the air unfit to breathe and the water unfit to drink). And whom can you offend? Yourself, someone else, the earth, the angels, and God.

Unless you have been foolish enough to make a habit of iniquity, you will have many chances to choose between what's good and what's not in the course of a lifetime. Angels were given that choice one time only. For those who chose evil, the ultimate punishment lasts forever. No second chance there. We can have the challenge, and joy, of choosing good over and over again. We also have the reassurance that, when we make the wrong choices, a sincerely contrite heart can win us God's total forgiveness and the opportunity to start again fresh, as long as we are alive. And we can learn to forgive ourselves and others who have offended us—not always an easy task, but one that helps us build moral courage and spiritual strength as we go along.

We'll need that courage and strength as time passes. For most of us, our bodies, once a source of real and legitimate pleasure—dancing, making love, playing touch football, sailing before the wind—will start to fail us as we grow old. Angels don't have to worry about heart attacks or the terrible pain of advanced arthritis or being completely paralyzed on one side following a stroke. They don't have hands and feet and joints and blood vessels and brains. It's not a pretty picture for us humans. Yet even here there's something for all of us that angels can't experience.

We're eligible for spiritual medals of honor. I'm sure you know people who have won these. I do. I have a friend who has been fighting against Parkinson's disorder, with the trembling hands, weak limbs, unsteady gait it produces, for over ten years now. He takes his medicine faithfully. He still goes to his office. He sees friends and goes to his country house on weekends. He loves history and archaeology, and only last year he flew to Mexico to see the Mayan ruins in the Yucatan. It's a struggle for him every inch of the way. At least twice a week he falls down but, with help, picks himself up again and goes on his way by himself. I recall once walking alongside him on a snowy day when suddenly he began to lose his balance. I put my arms around him to hold him up. He was dead weight. Together we fell into a snowbank, and we lay there, laughing (can you imagine, *laughing?*) for a couple of minutes until a nice lady came along and helped us both up.

It is said that when the end comes, when we die, an angel comes to take us to our new home. On television's *Touched by an Angel*, his name is Andrew. But most people who believe in angels think it's the archangel Michael who escorts us there. He must be a pretty busy angel. I suspect he has some help. But we have the chance to do our part, too, to make the effort to face the reality of death and to die with dignity. A couple of years before my own father died, he took me to the local undertaker and selected the casket in which he wanted to be buried. He knew I'd be very upset when he died, and he didn't want me, his only child, to be vulnerable to the pressures that he thought the morticians and other members of our family would put on me to do more. He was right. When the time came, I was asked how I could bury a man as prominent as my father had been in such a simple casket, and I was prepared to answer that it was the one that he himself had chosen. He also chose the particular place in the cemetery where he wanted himself and my mother eventually to be buried, and chose a headstone to mark the place.

He gets a medal of honor too, for being a model for me of how to face death with courage and faith. My dad believed very much in God, but I don't know what he thought of angels. The subject never came up. My mother believed, I know.

So you see, there's plenty of sadness and joy in this world to help us on our spiritual quest, and many an adventure on our way. Angels are here to guide and protect us. But not being human beings, they can only imagine how exciting it can be.

XV

Taking Care of Our Mortal Selves

In which you'll learn how to enjoy the best of both worlds

SINCE THERE are so many wonderful things about being human, we'd do well to use our angel strengths to take care of our bodies as well as our spirits. I am a physician, after all, and naturally this thought would occur to me, especially these days when we need all our wits about us to get the medical care we require, and when patients as well as doctors have more information than ever about how we can prevent illness and stay well.

What are the basic ingredients of health? You know most of them already: exercise; good nutrition; adequate sleep; safe and sane sex; avoiding harmful substances—cigarettes, illegal drugs, or too much whiskey; the successful management of stress; recognizing signs and symptoms of illness in its earliest stages and taking the steps necessary to get good medical care.

EXERCISE

Let's start with exercise. Angels are very powerful, but since they are spiritual beings, they don't have to exercise. We humans, with our muscles and circulatory systems, do. You can see the resurgence of interest in staying physically fit everywhere. Gyms are packed with men and women on treadmills and lifting weights. The streets are crowded with joggers running, panting, sweating, in the early morning hours.

Exercise is not only good for your heart and circulatory system. It builds muscular strength too. In fact, it helps your mind and spirit come alive. And you're never too old to start. I know a man whose only exercise during most of his life was walking a mile or two a day and swimming in the ocean. In his sixties he signed up for a program of aerobics and weights and now he leg-presses 170 pounds and pulls down 80, and he feels better than he has in years. That man is me.

DIET

Poor nutrition and obesity are two of the most serious health problems in America today. High blood pressure, elevated cholesterol levels, and overall sluggishness set the stage for heart attacks, stroke, and even cancer. What we all need is a fundamental commitment to achieving our optimal weight and to revising our eating habits to maintain ourselves at that level.

I, like everyone else, can experience a craving for a cheeseburger swathed in ketchup from time to time.

But I never cease to be amazed to watch the customers in fast food restaurants putting away huge portions of burgers and fries, doused in ketchup, with milkshakes on the side. I can only hope that they don't go there any more often than I do, and that they eat healthier foods at home, such as broccoli, carrots, green beans for which all of us can develop a taste. Even people who do eat right can benefit from taking vitamin supplements, since modern food processing frequently removes essential nutritional elements from even potentially wholesome foods.

Angels are lucky in that they don't have to worry about weight or nutritional problems. But their will and discipline can be an inspiration to us in our own efforts to be healthy. Incidentally, what do you think your guardian angel is thinking, watching you reach for that second helping of cherry pie?

A GOOD NIGHT'S SLEEP

We are meant to spend about a third of our lives asleep. It's a restorative experience. Few things are more delicious than a sound sleep lasting eight or nine hours, preferably starting before midnight, especially when the air is cool and a light breeze blows in through an open window. Yet the people who have sleep difficulties number in the tens of millions, and many have unfortunately become dependent on sleeping medications to help them get through the night. While it's true that some people have specific sleep disorders, such as sleep apnea, that can be properly diagnosed only in a sleep clinic, most people who have trouble sleeping are the victims of poor habits. They stay up until all hours, throwing their biological clocks out of whack, watching television in bed, mistakenly believing that it will help them feel sleepy. In fact it usually tends to do the very opposite. They drink coffee at dinner, ignoring the fact that caffeine's stimulation lasts more than ten hours, well past bedtime.

There are many simple things you can do to help you sleep better—stretching exercises in the late evening, reading a book, a glass of 1 percent milk, or a glass of purified water. Be sure your mattress is comfortable and your room is dark. I'm sure you've heard most of these suggestions before, and more as well. It's angel-like discipline that will get you to put them into regular practice.

Anxiety is one of the most common causes of insomnia. People are afraid to let themselves fall asleep for any number of reasons. They're afraid they'll miss out on something, as children often feel when they have to go to bed before their parents. Or they may fear unconsciousness itself, a state of total relaxation in which they are temporarily helpless to defend themselves against the terrors of the night. Maybe they lack faith that everything will be all right, and that they'll wake up safe and sound when morning comes. Maybe they have a need to control everything, and they cannot allow themselves to be out of control, even in the privacy of their own bedrooms.

Sleep requires you to be willing to allow something to happen that you cannot will. There may be a few people who can say to themselves: "Now I will sleep!" but I have yet to meet one. It's something you have to let happen. To do that, you must have your physical, psychological, and spiritual life in order. You have to trust yourself.

Trusting your angels can help too. If you have difficulty sleeping, you might try crawling under the covers and thinking peaceful and reassuring thoughts about the angels who will look after you throughout the night. And count angels as you doze off. Counting angels is probably a lot more effective than counting sheep.

MANAGING STRESS

Although a good deal of lip service is given to the notion that stress, or, more accurately, how well or poorly we manage stress, has a profound influence on our psychological and physical health, you'd be surprised how many people, doctors included, don't really take it very seriously. Only last year, a friend of mine collapsed and died of a heart attack, even though he had presumably been in excellent health up to that time. David was only forty-three years old. I knew him well, and I knew that he had never come to terms with a number of unresolved tensions in his life.

A pattern that researchers have established as significantly related to heart disease is finding yourself in a situation or a relationship that's frustrating, disheartening, and demoralizing, and feeling unable to change the way things are, change how you experience them, or escape them. David was an ambitious man who worked for a company that manufactured containers, those huge metal boxes that you see being loaded onto railroad trains and ships. He'd risen through the ranks as high as he could. Because the business was family-run, David's promotion to a position in senior management was not likely to happen. Meanwhile, his immediate boss was insensitive, rude, blaming, and indecisive. David dreaded going to work in the mornings and was utterly exhausted by the time he arrived home, often late for dinner. He tried to find another job or secure a transfer within his own company, to no avail.

What made his situation so desperate was the fact that he did not make the vital connection between his stressful situation and his health. He fumed inside, but he was too proud to talk with his wife or friends about his distress. It never occurred to him to seek out professional help. The door to his soul was locked tight. When everything exploded, it blew David's heart apart in the process.

David was frustrated and angry because he was caught in a predicament that he desperately wanted to escape but from which he saw no exit. Doctors have found a different scenario to be associated with the development of cancer: intensely desiring something or someone that you can never have. This is not to say that stress directly causes cancer. Viruses or chemicals probably affect cell metabolism to cause cancer. But stress suppresses your immune system, making you more vulnerable to disease.

For example, say you're going through a divorce you didn't initiate and don't want. You want your husband or wife back. But he or she adamantly rejects any possibility of reconciliation. You're immobilized. You can't let go. You can't bring yourself to start thinking about ways to rebuild your life. You are too embarrassed or feel too hopeless to talk things over with a friend or a professional. You are indeed at risk, although, unlike a heart attack, it may take time for cancer cells to start to multiply in your body.

I don't mean to scare anyone here. But we're talking about what we can learn from the angels to help us lead healthier and more adaptive lives. We can do that only by identifying areas of risk and cultivating angel-like qualities to help us overcome them. Knowledge and insight into the ramifications of what he was going through could have helped my friend David. Add a touch of humility and a willingness to talk things out with someone, and he might still be alive today. I don't really know whether he believed in God, but I do know that faith goes a long way in providing us with the strength and resilience necessary to deal with stress.

WHEN YOU NEED TO SEE THE DOCTOR

Ever since I was in my middle forties, I've seen my physician twice a year, once for a complete physical, and the second time for a brief checkup. I know too many people who never go to a doctor until they're really sick. Some are too lazy. Others operate on the premise that staying away from doctors gives them a better chance of staying well. They believe that what you don't know can't hurt you. Or they ask themselves,

What if I do have something wrong and they can't do anything about it, what then? No angel would think that way. They're too smart.

Some people used to tease me about being a bit of a hypochondriac, which I'm not. But that didn't deter me from my determination to stick to my schedule of semi-annual visits. No one teases me any more, not since my habit of seeing my doctor regularly allowed him to pick up early signs of prostate cancer, leading to timely treatment and, since a number of years have gone by since my surgery, hopefully a lasting cure.

Never before in this century has it been so imperative that we all take more personal responsibility for our health. Managed care has made it this way. So has the miraculous speed with which new medical breakthroughs are taking place. I have no doubt that if angels were faced with the kinds of health problems we humans are, they could do whatever was required to stay in good shape, consulting appropriate professionals on a regular basis, and they wouldn't be shopping around to see how they could pay the least amount of money for their care, regardless of quality. I'm sure that, once given a diagnosis, they would find out as much as they could about their condition and any treatments proposed. Nor would they hesitate to ask pertinent questions and expect answers in a language they could comprehend (which would be quite easy, since we're talking about angels here). They might even make some suggestions to their doctors, considering how smart they are and how effectively they communicate.

When it comes to decision-making time, I see them making informed choices about their treatments and complying meticulously with the regimens established for them. And if they didn't believe in those regimens, I'm sure they'd seek advice somewhere else.

Angels would behave in that sort of logical, disciplined way if they had to get medical help, which they obviously don't. But we do, and we'd be wise to follow their example.

Of course, some people insist that angels don't exist, never having seen one. And other people ask why they appear only to certain humans, though others still say that angels come to everyone. The question to ask is: Who will recognize them when they come?

A Book of Angels
SOPHY BURNHAM

XVI

Angel Recognition

For those who choose to be the guardians

I AM EIGHTEEN again. I am sitting in a dark room, watching small silhouettes appear on a white screen, one after the other in quick succession. I am not alone. Twenty other sailors are crowded together with me into this small space. Outside, the snow is piled ten feet high, and the temperature is five degrees below zero. Here inside, however, it is unbearably warm. I can hardly keep my head upright, and I fight against a powerful urge to fall asleep. It's aircraft recognition class. The men identify each plane and call out its name as its outline appears on the screen. Zero. Kate. Messerschmitt. Junker. P 47 Thunderbolt. F4U Corsair. B-29. One day, in the future, some of us will stand watch on the deck of a ship, staring at the clouds, searching, waiting to give a warning signal if enemy aircraft appear, protecting our own planes from being shot down by mistake. The slidemachine clicks mercilessly on. I am breathing heavily. My eyelids flutter. I pull myself erect and shake my hands on either side of me, upset that I've just misidentified another plane, one of our own, my third in a row.

Fifty years separate me from that room. Now, I've engaged in a different kind of observational task, standing on the deck of my life, trying to recognize angels and hoping I do a better job this time around than I did with airplanes.

What strikes me at first is how quickly the years have flown by. The past is a patchwork of memories, often with no rhyme or reason as to which come to mind easily and which seem forever lost. It is crowded with people—family, friends, colleagues, patients. It's full of events whose importance seems to have little bearing on how clearly I remember them. Going to Bamberger's department store with my mother for instance, and having lunch in the Ivy Tea Room and being served an ice cream cone, upside down in a dish, decorated with colorful candy to look like a clown. Or skating on a pond near home and holding hands with a girl from school as we moved across the ice ; I even remember her name: Vivian. Delivering the valedictory address at my college graduation. Sitting with one of my earliest patients in her hospital room, confused by the intelligent, delicately beautiful, soft-spoken young woman I saw, in contrast to the dire future my supervisor predicted for her. He proved to be right. I remember her name too; It was Mary. Watching my first son, Christopher, be born, and years later hugging each other goodbye at LaGuardia Airport as he went off to college. Deciding to push ahead with treatment for a patient of mine, which saved her sanity and her life, when all the consultants who had seen her considered her case hopeless. Talking with one of my oldest and best friends on the telephone after he'd had surgery, the day before he quite unexpectedly died. Being interviewed by Jane Pauley on television. Sitting for a photo with medical school friends at our fortieth reunion and thinking that they all looked very much as I remembered them from years ago. The Good Friday candlelight procession at St. Joan of Arc church on Cape Cod.

What strikes me now is the realization that angels were there. They were always there.

I shall never know the whole story. I shall never know how much of a role they played in my life. Angels, and life, are that way.

ANGEL PARALLELS

But in preparing to write this book, I not only have become more aware of the angels. I have also recognized the striking parallel between the tasks of angels and the work I carry out as a doctor and psychiatrist, although, to be sure, in a far less efficient manner. You could say that the psychiatrist's (or any doctor's or therapist's) job is to help people under his or her care to overcome human obstacles that stand in the way of their becoming more angel-like in spirit and behavior.

Consider will. Almost without exception, people who come to me do so at a time in their lives when they have lost some degree of control over their lives.

They're frightened and depressed. Or they're confused about choices they have to make. Or they are immobilized and unable to attend to the responsibilities of their lives with their usual effectiveness. It's my job to help restore their sense of freedom and regain mastery over their lives.

Knowledge. Patients need new ways to understand their lives. Therapists help our patients sort things out, discover the sources of their distress and resolve them, and identify their hidden strengths and encourage them.

Love. Patients often need to learn to be more generous. So does everyone. One way we help them do this is by doing it ourselves, by being models of honest caring. We're there not just to relieve their symptoms and set them back on course. We're there to encourage them to replace old habits of self-concern with new ones of concern for others. There's been a lot of talk about the idea of learning to love yourself. Be your own best friend. Love yourself first, then you will learn to love others. Well, why not turn that around? *Learn to love others, and in the process you'll learn to love yourself.*

Communication. These days, most of the people who come to see me chiefly complain of trouble with their relationships. A central factor in their difficulties is somebody's failure to communicate. Now, communicating happens to be the primary instrument in our medical armamentarium. Words and ideas and feelings are to therapists what scalpels and sponges and sutures are to surgeons. We use our own communication skills to help patients communicate more effectively themselves. And when we can help patients combine these skills with loving, understanding, and forgiving, we can help them be better able to successfully handle all (or most of) their interpersonal relationships.

Guiding and protecting. Just think about it. Whenever a patient comes to see a doctor or therapist, he or she is especially vulnerable. It's a rather helpless position to be in. One of our tasks is to protect our patients, from others, from themselves, even from us. *Noli nocere* means "do no harm"; as a basic ethic of medical practice, it goes back to the days of Hippocrates. Our second task is to set goals that will incorporate ways in which patients will find not only relief from their distress and solutions for their dilemmas but roads to follow to become more successful as human beings in years to come.

Healing. This is the heart of our work. Our patients are hurting. They have suffered psychic injury. Our strongest tool to help them is something they usually haven't found anywhere else. It's empathy. We reassure them by feeling *with* them. We try to make what they have been experiencing—until now a mystery to them—comprehensible. We help them overcome embarrassment and humiliation, regain perspective, and restore a sense of coherence.

Spirituality. Much as we might like to, this is one issue we cannot evade. Every patient has, or is in search of, some meaning to his or her life. The least we can do is to encourage a virtuous life for its own sake. But when we discover that spirituality is important to a patient, it is something we must respect and, if we are capable, nurture.

In other words, we are actually in the business of encouraging our patients to become more angel-like. And we do this by removing the obstacles that human conflict and vulnerability put in the way. Such obstacles can as often be physical as psychological. For example, when we prescribe medications that affect malfunctioning biological processes to relieve a depressive mood that just won't go away on its own, and which is often associated with a loss of energy, hope, and even faith at times, we are taking steps to enable patients to regain energy, hope, and even faith—to be able to learn more about how to develop angel strengths in their lives.

A FRIEND TO OTHERS. A FRIEND TO YOURSELF.

I've known for years that much of the time, *except for attending to the physical aspects of emotional distress*, anyone willing to take the time and make the effort to learn how can be his or her own therapist, and a therapist to others. I prefer the term "friend." A friend to others. A friend to yourself.

Many years ago I read a book called *What's the World Coming To?* It predicted that by the end of this century millions of people would be engaged in tending to the psychological and emotional needs of millions of other people. It looks as if that prediction has come true. But there's no reason why all these helpers, or even a significant number of them, need be professionals. It doesn't make any sense. And it's not going to happen.

You are going to have to do much of the work of relationships yourself. Indeed, it's best that way, because in your own efforts to introduce angel strengths into your life, you'll be doing the same for others. In your efforts to get others to introduce these strengths into their lives—by example, by sharing your thoughts and feelings on the subject, by compassion and encouragement—you will be strengthening those very qualities in yourself.

We shall not cease from exploration
And the end of all our exploring
Will be to arrive where we started
And know the place for the first time.

Little Gidding
T. S. ELIOT

Selected References

Allen, James. *As a Man Thinketh*. Peter Pauper Press. New York. 1983

Anderson, Joan Webster. *Where Angels Walk: True Stories of Heavenly Visitors*. Ballantine Books. New York. 1993.

Angels in Our Midst. Compiled by the Editors of Guideposts. Doubleday. New York. 1993

Burnham, Sophy. *A Book of Angels*. Ballantine Books. New York. 1990

Burton, Robert. *The Anatomy of Melancholy*. Various editions.

Campbell, Don. *The Mozart Effect*. Avon Books. New York. 1997

Carrol, Robert, and Stephen Prickett, Eds. *The Bible: Authorized King James Version* (World's Classics). Oxford University Press. New York. 1997

Eliot, T. S. *The Cocktail Party*. Harcourt, Brace and Company. New York. 1950

Flach, Frederic, MD. *Putting the Pieces Together Again*. Hatherleigh Press. New York. 1996

Flach, Frederic, MD. *Resilience*. Hatherleigh Press. New York. 1997

Giudici, Maria Pia. *The Angels*. Alba House. New York. 1995

Graham, Billy. *Angels*. Word Publishing. Dallas, Texas. 1975, 1995

Hanson, Jeanne K., *The Poetry of Angels*. Crown Trade Paperbacks. New York. 1995

Hiesberger, Jean Marie, Eds. *The Catholic Bible: New American Bible*. Oxford University Press. New York. 1995

Jung, Carl G. *Modern Man in Search of a Soul.* Translated by W. S. Bell and C. F. Payne. Harcourt Brace and Company, New York. 1955

Koenig, H. G., L.K. George, and B.L. Peterson. "Religiousity and Remission from Depression in Medically Older Patients." *American Journal of Psychiatry.* Volume 155: 536-542. 1998

Kreeft, Peter. *Angels (and Demons).* Ignatius Press. San Francisco. 1995

Lewis, James R., and Oliver, Evelyn Dorothy. Edited by Kelly S. Sisung. *Angels A to Z.* Visible Ink Press. Detroit, Michigan. 1996

Merton, Thomas. *Seeds of Contemplation.* Greenwood. Wilton, Connecticut. 1979

Milne, A. A. *The House at Pooh Corner.* E. P Dutton & Co. New York. 1928

Milne, A. A. *The Complete Tales of Winnie-the-Pooh.* New York: Penguin USA. New York. 1996

Moody, Raymond A., Jr. *Life After Life: The Investogation of a Phenomenon—Survival of Bodily Death.* Walker & Co. New York. 1988.

The Open Bible Expanded Editon: *New American Standard Bible.* Thomas Nelson Publishers. Nashville. 1985

Pickering, George. *Creative Malady.* Oxford University Press. New York. 1974

Saint-Exupéry, A de. *Flight to Arras.* Reynal & Hitchcock. New York. 1942

Siegal, B. S. *Love, Medicine, and Miracles.* Harper Collins. New York. 1986

Stevens, Wallace. *The Collected Poems of Wallace Stevens.* New York: Vintage Books. 1990

Watts, A. *Tao: The Watercourse Way.* Pantheon Books. New York 1975

About the Authors

DR. FREDERIC FLACH

A prominent New York psychiatrist and man of faith, Dr. Flach enriched the lives of many and was his own example of how to live spiritually in the modern world. Dr. Flach is the author of many books, including *The Secret Strength of Depression, Choices,* and *Faith, Healing and Miracles.*

JANICE T. CONNELL

Janice T. Connell is the author of several bestsellers, including *Meetings with Mary, Visions of the Children, Queen of the Cosmos, Triumph of the Immaculate Heart,* and *Angel Power.* She resides in Washington, DC, and Arizona and is a frequent radio commentator and guest speaker.

Angel Notes

_____

_____

_____

_____

_____

_____

_____

_____

_____

_____

_____

_____

_____

_____

_____

_____

_____

_____

_____

_____

_____

_____

_____

_____

_____

_____

_____

_____

_____

_____

_____

_____

_____

_____

_____

_____

_____

_____

_____

_____

_____

_____

_____